The UPWARD CALL

Studies in Christian Discipleship

John Coblentz

Christian Light Publications, Inc.
Harrisonburg, Virginia 22802

THE UPWARD CALL

Christian Light Publications, Inc., Harrisonburg, Virginia 22802
©1997 by Christian Light Publications, Inc.
Printed in the United States of America

Fourth Printing, 2005

Cover Design: David W. Miller

ISBN-13: 978-0-87813-567-7
ISBN-10: 0-87813-567-7

Foreword

The age of instant potatoes and microprocessors has not given us a speedy route to spiritual maturity. If anything, our penchant for speed has made us willing to settle for little or nothing in spiritual growth because the process is slow and difficult. Duties and schedule call for motion, action, and quick progress. We are too hurried and harried to sit long with Jesus.

But the way of discipleship is still a process. It is a process that takes time—a lifetime in fact. It is a process that calls us to stop, step out of hurry, sit down, meditate, and study. It is furthermore a process that involves us with our brothers and sisters in Christ, calls us to fellowship together, worship together, study together, and thus grow together.

This book is not a three-hour miracle course. It is a growth guide, a discipleship tool. The work is long, sometimes difficult, but always rewarding.

This book is designed to be used in a group, with older, more mature disciples leading younger ones— together discussing, challenging, asking—seeking to be changed into the likeness of Jesus. It certainly may be read and studied with much profit by yearning individuals also.

Each lesson begins with a personal inventory, designed to open the heart in honesty to the central truths of the lesson. This is followed by the Scriptures from which the lesson derives. Each passage is then looked at separately and commented upon. The Study Questions are intended to provide opportunity to further explore the passage and its bearing upon the lesson. At the end of each lesson is a list of questions directing disciples toward further application. Many of these questions do not call for right-wrong answers. They could be answered in different ways, depending on the student and his situation. That is what application is—a person who plants corn in Florida may use a different kind of seed and certainly a different schedule than a person who plants corn in North Dakota. The challenge facing every disciple is not merely to learn the principles of God's Word, but to live by them at home, in the workplace, in the market, and in the day-by-day relationships with other people.

The opening three lessons explore God's call to follow Jesus—what that call is and what it entails. The next six lessons get into the bone and sinew of living. Here we explore what we really are and what issues face every man and woman who would follow Jesus. The last three lessons lay before us the call to serve our fellowmen. The work God does in us becomes the means of His working out through us as we serve in His kingdom, building up other believers, and reaching the lost.

Some, no doubt, will want to rush through this study, get their instant growth, and go. But if you want real growth, take it slowly. Be honest. Be real. Face the issues. Face yourself. Face the Master. Answering the upward call takes time. It calls for courage. It demands discipline. But our upward walk has a destination. Up there, forever with Him, we will seize the prize, and every difficulty we faced here will seem as nothing!

—John Coblentz

Contents

PART I
UNDERSTANDING GOD'S CALL

Lesson 1: Disciples of Jesus Christ
Lesson 2: Members of Christ's Body
Lesson 3: Strangers in the World

"I press toward the mark for the prize of the high calling of God in Christ Jesus [the upward call of God, NASB]" (Philippians 3:14).

The world drags us downward. The devil tempts us downward. Our own desires exert a continual downward pull. It is *God* who calls us upward through His Son, Christ Jesus.

God the Son came down and lived among us. He offered us an alternative to this world—Himself. He conquered the devil and broke all his powers by a glorious resurrection from the dead. This Son of God asks us to forsake the world, resist the devil, surrender our entire being to Him, and *come and follow Him.*

This is an upward call! It is a lifelong climb. It is a discipleship after Jesus Christ, a life lived in communion with Him, being completely under His direction. It is a glorious ascent that will one day burst into the eternal realms of light where we will be at home forever with the One we followed on earth.

The first three lessons of this study will take us to the Bible to understand the heart of God's call. What does He really expect from us? We will learn that God calls us to be disciples of Jesus, that this call brings us into the assembly of other disciples (the church), and that this call sets us apart from the world.

Lesson 1

Disciples of Jesus Christ

INTRODUCTION

Many today claim to be Christians who have little understanding of what it means actually to follow Jesus. They want to share the benefits of Christianity, want to claim the promises of the Bible, want to go to heaven when they die, but live the majority of their lives without regard to Christ. Are they disciples of Jesus? Are they Christians? The goal of this study will not be to make you judges of others, but to challenge you to discipleship and to give you a base for challenging others to discipleship.

The truth is that a man would only be fooling himself if he claimed to be a farmer but spent 90 percent of his time and effort doing other things, and if his 10 percent "involvement" in farming was only passive—listening to others talk about it, thinking about it, talking about it, but never actively farming. Many similarly are deceived today about their "Christianity" because they spend several hours a week in church where they listen to the preacher, make a few comments in Sunday school, give an offering, visit with other church members afterward, and go home.

Such Christianity offers little relationship with Jesus, allows much worldliness (even under the guise of a "separated" life), and is largely impotent in reaching the lost. It is not a life of discipleship.

PERSONAL INVENTORY

1. How would you rate the general discipleship concepts in your religious environment?
   a. strong   b. average   c. needing help   d. sick

2. If your answer above is not a., what do you think are major reasons for the situation?
   a. lack of understanding   b. spiritual deception
   c. worldly influences   d. false doctrine
   e. (other) _____ all of the above! _____

3. How would you rate your own discipleship?
   a. strong   b. untaught   c. backslidden
   d. average   e. miserable   f. not sure

4. In a few sentences: (a) describe your commitment to Jesus as it presently stands, and (b) state what you would like to learn about discipleship.

My comm. is to walk daily with the Lord by reading his word, spending time in prayer, sharing with others.

SCRIPTURAL BACKGROUND

And Jesus, walking by the sea of Galilee, saw two brethren, Simon called Peter, and Andrew his brother, casting a net into the sea: for they were fishers. And he saith unto them, Follow me, and I will make you fishers of men. And they straightway left their nets, and followed him. And going on from thence, he saw other two brethren, James the son of Zebedee, and John his brother, in a ship with Zebedee their father, mending their nets; and he called them. And they immediately left the ship and their father, and followed him. Matthew 4:18-22.

The disciple is not above his master, nor the servant above his lord. It is enough for the disciple that he be as his master, and the servant as his lord. Matthew 10:24, 25a.

And he said to them all, If any man will come after me, let him deny himself, and take up his cross daily, and follow me. For whosoever will save his life shall lose it: but whosoever will lose his life for my sake, the same shall save it. For what is a man advantaged, if he gain the whole world, and lose himself, or be cast away? Luke 9:23-25.

And there went great multitudes with him: and he turned, and said unto them, If any man come to me, and hate not his father, and mother, and wife, and children, and brethren, and sisters, yea, and his own life also, he cannot be my disciple. And whosoever doth not bear his cross, and come after me, cannot be my disciple. So likewise, whosoever he be of you that forsaketh not all that he hath, he cannot be my disciple. Luke 14:25-27, 33.

UNDERSTANDING THE SCRIPTURES

> *And Jesus, walking by the sea of Galilee, saw two brethren, Simon called Peter, and Andrew his brother, casting a net into the sea: for they were fishers. And he saith unto them, Follow me, and I will make you fishers of men. And they straightway left their nets, and followed him. And going on from thence, he saw other two brethren, James the son of Zebedee, and John his brother, in a ship with Zebedee their father, mending their nets; and he called them. And they immediately left the ship and their father, and followed him.* Matthew 4:18-22.

OBSERVATION #1: Jesus called some to follow Him in a teacher/learner relationship during His earthly ministry.

For these disciples, this meant leaving their earthly businesses and devoting themselves to the life He lived. Simon, Andrew, James, and John left the fishing trade to become disciples of Jesus. This included spending time with Him, hearing His teaching, obeying His instructions, and following His example.

OBSERVATION #2: Following Jesus is more important than one's earthly livelihood.

Jesus nowhere indicates that everyone must leave his trade to follow Him, but Jesus' call to such as Peter and Andrew does tell us that discipleship is more important than business. Some business might be left because it is wrong, or it involves us in wrong. But the business of fishing, as far as we know, was an upright occupation. Jesus had work for the men that was higher—"I will make you fishers of men." We can assume that today, discipleship continues to be more important than business. We can also assume that Jesus will call some to forsake business, not because it is wrong, but because there is other work, higher work, to be done.

OBSERVATION #3: Work in behalf of the souls of people is a higher work than earthly business.

Again, it was not wrong to be a fisherman. But in asking Peter and Andrew to give up fishing on the sea to become fishers of men, Jesus was asking one to yield to the other. As we ponder Jesus' words, we wonder why kingdom work is not more valued today. From other Scriptures we realize that not all disciples went into full-time evangelism. Even notable evangelists like Paul worked a trade at times in conjunction with kingdom work. (See Acts 18:3; 2 Thessalonians 3:8-10.) But Christians should regard work for the souls of men as noble work, as a privilege, and should desire to be involved in such work wherever possible and to support others in such work.

Study Questions

1. What did Jesus' call to Andrew, Peter, James, and John mean for them? What was their response? What changes do you think Jesus' call brought into their lives?

2. What did Jesus mean when He said, "I will make you fishers of men"?

3. How do we understand the relative value of fishing for fish and fishing for men? How might we become imbalanced in this?

4. Are there other examples either in the Bible or in your experience where discipleship meant giving up one's business?

5. How do we know that working in full-time church work does not necessarily relieve us of work in a trade?

> *The disciple is not above his master, nor the servant above his lord. It is enough for the disciple that he be as his master, and the servant as his lord.* Matthew 10:24, 25a.

OBSERVATION #4: In the teacher/learner relationship, the teacher is the master.

The teacher is in charge. The teacher gives the directions. The teacher instructs the learner. This is the relationship. The learner, therefore, must be humble, teachable, obedient, meek, and responsive. He must tune his ears as one whose life is under the command of another. His role is not to correct or instruct his master, but to listen and follow.

OBSERVATION #5: The goal of discipleship is to make the followers like the Master.

A master/learner relationship was more common in Jesus' day than in ours. Neither the modern school system nor the modern workplace offers an exact parallel to the master/learner relationship of Jesus' day. The role of the disciple was not merely to learn a set of precepts, but to learn a way of life. Jesus did not want His followers merely to memorize what He knew, but to become like He was. The goal of the disciple was to become like the Master. We may assume that today Jesus continues to desire His disciples to spend time with Him, not merely to acquaint themselves with His teachings or to know the history of His life, but to know Him and be devoted to becoming like Him.

Study Questions

1. What is the relationship between the master and the disciple?

2. Who is our master?

3. What characteristics must be ours to have a proper relationship with Jesus?

4. What is the goal of the disciple?

5. How is the disciple/master relationship different from modern schooling?

6. How do we know that Jesus was effective with His disciples in the master/disciple relationship?

> *And he said to them all, If any man will come after me, let him deny himself, and take up his cross daily, and follow me. For whosoever will save his life shall lose it: but whosoever will lose his life for my sake, the same shall save it. For what is a man advantaged, if he gain the whole world, and lose himself, or be cast away? Luke 9:23-25.*

OBSERVATION #6: There is a following after Jesus which is required of all believers.

We have seen how Jesus called certain disciples to literally follow Him around while He was on earth. The above call, however, is one that goes out to "all," to "whosoever." It is a call that comes to you today.

OBSERVATION #7: Following Jesus involves denying yourself.

Jesus lays the ax to the root. He says in effect: "I insist on an unconditional surrender of your life to My authority. I am not asking for half of your time, for 90 percent of your savings, or for two years of your life. I want you. I demand that every high thing in your life that exalts itself against Me be uncovered, disowned, and turned over. I ask that every excuse against My control in your life be torn up and burned. I require that you renounce every good thing in your life that you have used as a bargaining tool against My will. Turn over the whole self—your desires, your plans, your friendships, your reading, your reputation, your past, your present, your future—the whole package. I insist on everything because anything you keep—no matter how harmless or trivial or good it appears to you—represents an affront to My throne. No one who follows Me serves two masters. I have not prepared a suburb of My kingdom for rebels—not one street, not the smallest corner. My followers trust Me completely and follow Me unreservedly."

Every man and woman who would follow Jesus must grapple with the harsh reality that in his own heart—at the core of his self—is a seat of rebellion against heaven. We want to run our own life, do our own thing, follow our own plans, go our own way. Jesus is simple and clear in this matter: you cannot follow Him unless you deny yourself. No one should ever be encouraged to "receive Jesus" or "become a Christian" on terms any less than absolute surrender. The heart of man must be turned over to the rule of heaven or it returns to the ways of sin and patterns of anarchy, and is deceived into thinking that it has a clear title to heaven even while hanging on to a life of sin. There is no such thing as receiving Jesus as Saviour, and sometime later, receiving Him as Lord. He is Lord, and he must be confessed as such for salvation (Romans 10:9). No one can follow Him and reserve the right to direct his own life. "If any man will come after me, let him *deny himself.*"

OBSERVATION #8: *Following Jesus involves taking up a cross daily.*

What does this mean? What is our cross? For Jesus, the cross was the suffering He experienced in obedience to the Father. Those who follow Jesus in a world of sin will face difficulty. There will be opposition. There will be some who mock, some who argue, some who lash out, some who hate. The follower of Jesus must settle it in his heart from the beginning: he will accept whatever suffering lies in the path of obedience to Jesus. Those who would mock the Master will mock the disciple. Those who reject the Master will reject the disciple. Those who crucified the Master would surely crucify the disciple. There is a cross for everyone who will follow Jesus.

OBSERVATION #9: *Sparing oneself of the cross amounts to forfeiting one's life eternally.*

"Whosoever will save his life shall lose it." The natural man shrinks from the cross, avoiding the suffering, the shame, and the death. Here again is the reason we must deny (wholly renounce) self. While self is on the throne, we will not receive the cross. A disciple of Jesus must care nothing for his reputation, his possessions, his comfort, or his life. He is following Jesus, and everything must be sacrificed to that pursuit.

OBSERVATION #10: *No amount of earthly gain, earthly pleasure, or earthly position is worth forfeiting one's soul.*

The devil offered power, position, and earthly wealth to Jesus if He would step out of the Father's plan. Jesus said, "Get thee hence!" The Father's plan took Jesus to the cross, but it likewise delivered Him from it. The devil's offer would have spared Jesus the cross, but what horrors would have followed! If we want to get out of this world alive, if we want to escape the judgment coming upon the whole universe, we must follow Jesus. He will lead us out. But all along the way, Satan will tempt us to avoid the suffering, to skip the cross; he will tantalize us with the world, with ego pleasers, with pleasures. *Nothing* he offers will compare to the glory that shall be revealed in the life to come. *Everything* he offers will turn to ruin in the end.

Study Questions

1. To whom comes Jesus' call, "Follow Me"?

2. What does it mean to deny self? Why is it important to deny self in order to follow Jesus?

3. How do modern theories about salvation disregard Jesus' teaching here?

4. Who is the cross for? What is the cross for followers of Jesus?

5. How do people try to spare themselves from the cross? What are the results of "saving one's life" in this way?

6. How did Satan offer Jesus an escape from the cross? What would have been the results if Jesus had yielded to Satan's suggestion?

7. How can we fortify ourselves against the temptations of Satan to avoid the cross?

> *And there went great multitudes with him: and he turned, and said unto them, If any man come to me, and hate not his father, and mother, and wife, and children, and brethren, and sisters, yea, and his own life also, he cannot be my disciple. And whosoever doth not bear his cross, and come after me, cannot be my disciple. So likewise, whosoever he be of you that forsaketh not all that he hath, he cannot be my disciple.* Luke 14:25-27, 33.

OBSERVATION #11: Relationship with Jesus is the supreme relationship.

The loyalty Jesus calls for is absolute. The directions He gives are life-saving. Jesus' words are strong words—"If any man come to me, and hate not his father . . . he cannot be my disciple." But the position of the Master in our heart is a matter of life or death, a matter of heaven or hell. As disciples of Jesus, we must be prepared to despise anyone or anything that would stand as a threat to the devotion we render to Jesus. Jesus Himself demonstrated this. He loved Peter in the proper sense, but when Peter tried to dissuade Him from the suffering of the cross, Jesus turned away from Peter as from the devil himself. "Get thee behind me, Satan: thou art an offence unto me: for thou savourest not the things that be of God, but those that be of men." (See Matthew 16:21-23.) As disciples, we must have such a surpassing love for the Master that all other loves are as hate in comparison.

OBSERVATION #12: *For everyone who would follow Jesus, something in his life will stand in his way as a barrier.*

Jesus asks "whosoever" comes after Him to forsake "all that he hath." The word is *all* because of our tendency to give up things that don't matter and retain something that does matter to us. The heart of Ananias and Sapphira is in all of us, to give a partial offering as though it were the whole, while retaining something for ourselves. The subtle thing about this is that the particular hang-up may vary for each individual. Some people never go to movies or dances or bars but listen regularly to the world's music. Others may rant against the world's music and all other worldly entertainment but secretly smile at their stockpiles of investments, never considering that Jesus gave specific directions for management of wealth. Anyone who has anything in his life that he would not give up unreservedly for Christ is barred from discipleship. He is withholding something from the lordship of Jesus.

OBSERVATION #13: *The call to be a follower of Jesus comes to us no matter what our station in life.*

Earlier we noted that Jesus called some to leave their earthly business to pursue heaven's business full time. We also acknowledged that not everyone is called to leave their earthly business—it is not necessarily wrong, in other words, to have jobs as fishermen, carpenters, farmers, etc. But inasmuch as *all* are called to follow Jesus *all the time* in *all things*, then ALL OF LIFE becomes a discipleship process. In this sense, the disciple has no secular life apart from his service life. Everywhere he is, he is a servant of Jesus. If the Lord does not call him away from carpentering, he serves the Lord in his carpentering. He listens to the voice of Jesus to direct his work. He considers how he might make his earthly work more of a heavenly blessing. His Christianity is not limited to a Sunday morning; it is a walk with Jesus, planning, deciding, relating, working in cooperation with the direction of the Lord every day.

Study Questions

1. What did Jesus say we need to do to be His disciple? How do we "hate" those close to us in the proper sense?

2. How did Jesus demonstrate this in His relationship with Peter?

3. What does Jesus call us to forsake in following Him?

4. What is our tendency in the matter of forsaking?

5. What are particular things people may have difficulty forsaking? What tactics do we use to avoid forsaking certain things?

6. Finish this statement: "Anyone who has something in his life he would not give up unreservedly _____ ." Why is it important to understand this?

7. Does the Lord call everyone to leave earthly business? What are the implications of including all of life in our discipleship?

APPLYING THE SCRIPTURE

1. Make a list of the specific things disciples of Jesus in the New Testament left behind to follow Him. (Include anyone, not just the 12 apostles; be specific.)

2. Do a survey. What percentage of people in your congregation have left earthly business to work for the souls of men?

3. What are specific ways we can make earthly business a blessing to the kingdom of heaven? Name some ways you have observed other Christians doing this.

4. What are some questionable businesses? What businesses advance the kingdom of God?

5. Make a list of statements in the Scripture regarding the lordship of Jesus. What observations can you make from these statements?

6. The goal of discipleship is that the followers become like the Master. Make a list of values Jesus lived by. Try to state the goals of Jesus' life. As you look at these lists, identify those in which you need to grow to be like Jesus.

7. What evidences have you observed that people are taught to receive Christ without denying themselves?

8. Do a study of the word deny in the original language. What does it mean? What does it imply?

9. What are evidences in a person's life that he has denied self? What are evidences that people have not denied self?

10. Can you name specific ways you have suffered for your obedience to Jesus?

11. List some specific times you have avoided suffering or shame. Are you willing to take this list before the Lord in prayer, making clear confession, denying yourself, and asking Him to be your teacher in these areas?

12. Do a study of suffering in the New Testament. Consider these questions: What was the attitude of the early church toward suffering? What kind of suffering did they experience? What were the results of their suffering? Make a list of the insights you gain from this study. How does your own view of suffering square with the Biblical view?

13. Make a list of things people commonly have trouble forsaking (things they want to retain control over in their lives).

14. What in your life has been difficult to forsake? Think carefully and prayerfully. Is there anything you do or own that you would not give up if asked by Jesus to do so? Name anything the Spirit of God brings to your mind. What do you sense Jesus saying to you about these things?

Members of Christ's Body

INTRODUCTION

Following Jesus Christ is not a private matter. Each disciple of Jesus walks in company with other disciples. Each disciple becomes a member of the group of disciples called the church (literally, "assembly") and begins to work together with the other disciples under the direction of Jesus. Discipleship, therefore, is not simply learning to follow Jesus, but learning to follow Him together with others who are following Him.

The church is not a material building but an assembly of spiritual people. Having church is not necessarily having a meeting but having a living relationship together with Christ. Just as a body has many members (eyes, hands, feet) and coordinates to do what the head directs, the church has many members, and those members must work together in coordination to accomplish what Jesus intends.

Having a building and having meetings in that building certainly can benefit the church. However, when church is understood primarily as a building or the meetings in a certain building, Christianity becomes shallow. God has called us into the church, into the assembly that follows Jesus. Everyone who would become a disciple of Jesus must not only accept his fellow disciples but also learn to work in cooperation with them under Christ.

A study of the church could become very involved. In this lesson, we will focus on how a Biblical understanding of the church is important to discipleship.

PERSONAL INVENTORY

1. Are you a member of a local fellowship of believers?

2. If your answer is yes, how much have you valued that membership?
   a. very important   b. somewhat beneficial
   c. optional   d. unimportant

3. If your answer to question #1 is no, what are your plans?

4. In a few sentences try to state your concept of church. Have you seen it as a building, the meetings, the people of God, or a combination of these?

5. Do you feel comfortable with the general attitudes toward the church among the Christians with whom you fellowship? Explain.

SCRIPTURAL BACKGROUND

And I say also unto thee, That thou art Peter, and upon this rock I will build my church; and the gates of hell shall not prevail against it. Matthew 16:18.

Then they that gladly received his word were baptized: and the same day there were added unto them about three thousand souls. And they continued stedfastly in the apostles' doctrine and fellowship, and in breaking of bread, and in prayers. Acts 2:41, 42.

For as the body is one, and hath many members, and all the members of that one body, being many, are one body: so also is Christ. . . . If the foot shall say, Because I am not the hand, I am not of the body; is it therefore not of the body? . . . If the whole body were an eye, where were the hearing? If the whole were hearing, where were the smelling? But now hath God set the members every one of them in the body, as it hath pleased him. . . . That there should be no schism in the body; but that the members should have the same care one for another. 1 Corinthians 12:12-25.

And hath put all things under his [Christ's] feet, and gave him to be the head over all things to the church, which is his body. Ephesians 1:22, 23.

From whom the whole body fitly joined together and compacted by that which every joint supplieth, according to the effectual working in the measure of every part, maketh increase of the body unto the edifying of itself in love. Ephesians 4:16.

21

UNDERSTANDING THE SCRIPTURES

> *And I say also unto thee, That thou art Peter, and upon this rock I will build my church; and the gates of hell shall not prevail against it.* Matthew 16:18.

OBSERVATION #1: *Jesus has purposed to build the church despite opposition.*

In the context of this verse, we find that Peter had just made a confession of Jesus as the Christ, the Son of God. That confession came after many days of discipling Peter. It was a revelation, not from man, but from God. As far as we know, this was the first time any of the disciples had verbalized the confession necessary for entrance into the church. The growth of the church depends upon bringing people to this same confession. We know that the enemy will do all he can to blind people to the truth about Jesus and to cause unbelievers to hate that truth, but we have the assurance that Jesus will build His church. He will bring stone after stone to rest upon the foundation that will never be destroyed.

Concerning "this rock," notice that the question in focus is "Who is Jesus?" (Matthew 16:13). Peter acknowledged that Jesus was the Christ, the Son of God. In the Greek, the name *Peter* means "little rock." The word Jesus used here for *rock* means "giant rock." Peter was a little rock who found *The Rock* over whom many stumble but upon whom the church is built. See Acts 4:11, 12 (Peter's own words); 1 Corinthians 3:11; and Ephesians 2:20.

Study Questions

1. What question had Jesus asked His disciples?
   Who do people say he is?

2. What reply had Peter given?
   Christ - the Son of the living God

3. What did Jesus say was the source of Peter's understanding? *The Father*

4. What did Peter's name mean? How was this in contrast to the word rock that Jesus said He would build His church on? *Little rock -*

5. What is the "rock" upon which the church is built? *Jesus*

6. What does each person need to do who comes into the church (as shown in this context)?
   Confess Jesus Christ

7. How does the enemy oppose the building of the church?

8. How do these words of Jesus give us assurance?
   He will build the church. The enemy will not prevail against it.

> *Then they that gladly received his word were baptized: and the same day there were added unto them about three thousand souls. And they continued stedfastly in the apostles' doctrine and fellowship, and in breaking of bread, and in prayers. Acts 2:41, 42.*

OBSERVATION #2: In the early church, becoming a follower of Jesus included receiving baptism whereby the believer joined the other followers of Jesus.

After the church was born, every person who came to Jesus came into the church, the assembly of believers. Repentance from sin, faith in Christ, and confession of Jesus as God's Son were entrance requirements; baptism was the entrance rite. Although church organization and structure were not in focus in the early days of the church, it is clear the believers knew who was "in" and who was not. The "number of names together were about an hundred and twenty" (Acts 1:15), when the Holy Spirit was poured out. To them were added on the Day of Pentecost "about three thousand souls" (Acts 2:41). "And the Lord added to the church daily such as should be saved" (Acts 2:47). After the hypocrisy of Ananias and Sapphira was exposed, "of the rest durst no man join himself to them." Still, "believers were the more added to the Lord, multitudes both of men and women" (Acts 5:13, 14). When Saul the persecutor, however, "assayed to join himself to the disciples" at Jerusalem, they held him off until Barnabas assured them Saul was a true believer. Then "he was with them coming in and going out at Jerusalem" (Acts 9:26-28). These Scriptures demonstrate that the church was concerned about knowing who belonged and who did not.

OBSERVATION #3: *The regular spiritual and social interaction of the early church focused on the discipleship of believers.*

In the Book of Acts the disciples became disciplers. The believers assembled regularly, and regularly the apostles taught them. Regularly they all fellowshipped together, and regularly they prayed. We get the decided impression that Jesus was the topic of conversation, getting to know Him was the desire of every heart, acquaintance with His teachings and remembrance of His death and resurrection were the heartbeat of every meeting. In such a context, discipleship was effective.

Study Questions

1. How many were added to the disciples of Jesus on the Day of Pentecost?

2. Do a study in the opening chapters of Acts. How many times can you find references to "the number of the disciples" or similar concepts? What does this teach us about the membership concepts of the early church?

3. Why was it important for the early church to know who was in and who was not?

4. What was the process by which believers were added to the church?

5. Why was Saul not immediately received into the church at Jerusalem?

6. What was the purpose of the church gatherings in the early church?

7. How did the focus of their talk correspond to discipleship? Can you find verses in Acts verifying that Jesus was the focus of their teaching?

> *For as the body is one, and hath many members, and all the members of that one body, being many, are one body: so also is Christ. . . . If the foot shall say, Because I am not the hand, I am not of the body; is it therefore not of the body? . . . If the whole body were an eye, where were the hearing? If the whole were hearing, where were the smelling? But now hath God set the members every one of them in the body, as it hath pleased him. . . . That there should be no schism in the body; but that the members should have the same care one for another.* 1 Corinthians 12:12-25.

OBSERVATION #4: In the church, there is diversity of function among members, but unity of purpose.

Like the human body, the church has a variety of members. Some are responsible to oversee, some to teach, some to help, some to discern, some to manage finances. This calls for diversity. And just as the Lord has equipped the various members of a natural body for a variety of operations, so He equips the various members of Christ's body with different gifts. Some receive the Spirit's power to do one thing, some to do another. The diversity of function however, becomes unity of purpose as each member works under the same Head. Although the hand does not see, it can work toward the same goal as the eye. In the body of Christ, the primary goal is to glorify God (1 Corinthians 10:31). Another important goal is the edification of the body. Spiritual gifts are given expressly for that purpose (1 Corinthians 12:7). These goals become the uniting factor for all members.

OBSERVATION #5: *The members of the church need each other.*

Jesus has a relationship with each member of His body, and He has purposes for each individual member. The work He has given to the church, however, takes collective working together. No one member can do it by himself. He needs his brothers and sisters working with him. Many people today focus on the power and possibilities of the Spirit-filled believer. The example of the early church tells us to focus on the power and possibilities of a Spirit-filled assembly of believers. Members in the church need one another. They simply cannot function as Christ intended unless they are joined to their fellow members and working in cooperation with them.

The need of members for each other, however, is not simply that they can be more productive. The members need each other for the care, the protection, and the nurture that only the collective setting can provide. Each believer has personal needs. He needs balance. He needs maturity. He needs purging. He needs wisdom. God doesn't intend that we find these needs fully met privately. Certainly, He gives us insight and growth and purging in our closets. But He intends that these needs be met also in the church. Thus, we need each other not only to do what Christ asks us to do but also to be what Christ wants us to be.

Study Questions

1. Explain how unity and diversity mesh in the proper concept of the church. Based on 1 Corinthians 12, how might unity and diversity be misunderstood to the detriment of the church?

2. List the gifts of the Spirit mentioned in 1 Corinthians 12. What do the last verses of the chapter teach us about diversity?

3. In practical terms, how might a church member insist on everyone being a "hand" or a "foot"?

4. What are some of the purposes that unite the church? Find verses that state these purposes.

5. How will a Spirit-filled person feel toward his brothers and sisters? How does the focus today often miss the importance of the collective body being Spirit-filled? What are the effects of this wrong focus?

6. What are some of the personal benefits a member should find in being joined to the body of believers? Based on that, what are the effects of a person distancing himself from the church?

And hath put all things under his [Christ's] feet, and gave him to be the head over all things to the church, which is his body. Ephesians 1:22, 23.

OBSERVATION #6: *Jesus' relationship to the church is one of complete authority.*

By His resurrection, Jesus was lifted to a position of authority that includes being "head over all things to the church." Every disciple of Jesus must individually hear Jesus' authoritative call to deny himself, to hate his own life, and to forsake all that he has. That absolute submission of each disciple is the groundwork for the absolute obedience of the church. As each member owns the lordship of Jesus, the whole church is prepared to do His will, come what may. The obedient church is a powerful church, and a powerful church disciples effectively.

Study Questions

1. What is Jesus' relationship to the church? Who gave Him that position? (See the context.) When was He given that position?

2. Explain the relationship between individual obedience to Christ and collective obedience.

3. What is the relationship between an obedient church and effective discipleship?

> *From whom the whole body fitly joined together and compacted by that which every joint supplieth, according to the effectual working in the measure of every part, maketh increase of the body unto the edifying of itself in love.* Ephesians 4:16.

OBSERVATION #7: Under Christ, every member is to contribute by love to the building up of the body.

We noted earlier that each member needs the body. Here we focus on the other side of the same point. Each member needs to sense his responsibility to help the other members. Edification must be a work of love. As someone has aptly said, "People don't care how much you know until they know how much you care."

Unfortunately, attempts to edify may easily be motivated by selfish interests. We grow impatient with fellow believers—"Would you please grow up!" is our inner feeling. We become eager to serve in order to be noticed for our talents—"Here I am to do a tremendous work for you. Everyone had better notice!" Or we serve others because we want to have certain people for our friends. If this is our motivation, we will be selective in our service, singling out certain people and avoiding others. LOVE forbids these selfish motivations. Jesus wants us to edify one another because of genuine love. His own life is our example.

OBSERVATION #8: The effective building up of the body yields a group maturity.

Discipleship and maturity are not simply to occur in individuals. Ephesians 4:16 is the culmination of a passage that describes group maturity. "Till we all come in the unity of the faith, and of the knowledge of the Son of God, unto a perfect man, unto the measure of the stature of the fulness of Christ" (v. 13). Although each Christian is to radiate Christ, it actually takes the assembly of believers to adequately demonstrate the "stature of Christ." The most powerful call to unbelievers is not the testimony of a Christian alone, but the testimony of the brotherhood of believers. The goal of discipling believers is that the church might experience maturity, because as the church demonstrates maturity, Christ is effectively made known to the world.

Study Questions

1. Read Ephesians 4:16 in other translations. What additional insights do you get?

2. What is expected of every member? How is every member equipped for that responsibility?

3. Finish this quote: "People don't care how much you know _____ ." In your own words, tell what this means.

4. How can people be motivated by selfish interests in helping others? Can you list other examples besides those given here?

5. What kind of maturity is described in Ephesians 4:13?

6. Why does it take the assembly of believers to demonstrate Christ accurately? (List as many reasons as you can.) What are the implications of this concept? How does it affect our view of discipleship?

APPLYING THE SCRIPTURE

1. Looking at the opening chapters of Acts, we realize that it was some years in the life of the early church before we have record of the church reaching out into other areas. Believers were being added to the church, but apparently not as a result of systematic church outreach. The apostles focused their energies on discipling the believers, on bringing the church to maturity. Why do you think this was necessary, and what can we learn from their example?

2. How did the needs of the early church change with time (compare, for example, Acts 2-4 with Acts 15), and what can we learn from this?

3. What are some of the ways Satan is using today to keep people from confessing Jesus as Lord and Saviour?

4. What are some methods of discipleship in the church that you have observed to be effective, and what are some you have seen as ineffective?

5. How do we know when we are being effective in discipleship?

6. What are some ways churches have experienced diversity of purpose to the point of no longer being effective?

7. List some specific ways other members have contributed to your spiritual maturity in the church.

8. Take a list of spiritual gifts in the New Testament (such as 1 Corinthians 12:8-10) and write a sentence or two about the importance of

each gift in the development of the church. What would have been the effect on the church if one were missing? Note: Some of the sign gifts were given by God specifically to establish the verity of the Gospel among unbelievers (1 Corinthians 14:22 and Acts 2).

9. After studying this lesson, do you feel you have had a proper value of the church in your own discipling experience? Have there been places where you have balked at being shaped by the other members in the church?

10. What level of commitment do you think Christ wants from the members of His body? Do you see that level of commitment in your congregation? Have you demonstrated that level of commitment yourself?

11. Imagine every member in your congregation having as his number one purpose to disciple others for Christ in love. List some specific results of such a situation.

12. What selfish motivations have you seen demonstrated in the work of the church? What selfish motivations have you personally struggled with? How would love operate differently?

13. What are some specific areas today where you feel the church is not demonstrating submission to the lordship of Christ? What are the effects?

Lesson 3

Strangers in the World

INTRODUCTION

"Wherefore come out from among them, and be ye separate, saith the Lord, and touch not the unclean thing; and I will receive you, And will be a Father unto you, and ye shall be my sons and daughters, saith the Lord Almighty" (2 Corinthians 6:17, 18).

Christ and the world stand at opposite poles. It is no more possible to follow Christ *and* the world than it is for a person to stand with one foot on the North Pole and one on the South Pole. When God calls people to Himself, therefore, He calls for separation from the world. There must be a coming *out* in order to experience an entrance *into*.

The coming out from the world, however, must be coupled with a coming unto God, or we simply end with being strange, not godly. There are many strange people in this world who are still ungodly.

This is a lesson, therefore, that cannot be studied safely by itself. Coming out, separation, strangers— these are inescapable aspects of the call of God. But they must be understood in the context of the call *to*

God, or they become pointless exercises in estrangement and are altogether void of life.

PERSONAL INVENTORY

1. What has been your attitude toward separation from the world?

2. What are some of the ways the world has been attractive to you in the past? *the lust of the eye...*

3. Do you feel you have been successful in viewing yourself as a stranger in this world, or do you tend to forget?

4. Make a list of questions you have now or have had about separation from the world.

SCRIPTURAL BACKGROUND

I have given them thy word; and the world hath hated them, because they are not of the world, even as I am not of the world. I pray not that thou shouldest take them out of the world, but that thou shouldest keep them from the evil. John 17:14, 15.

Be ye not unequally yoked together with unbelievers: for what fellowship hath righteousness with unrighteousness? and what communion hath light with darkness? And what concord hath Christ with Belial? or what part hath he that believeth with an infidel? And what agreement hath the temple of God with idols? for ye are the temple of the living God; as God hath said, I will dwell in them, and walk in them; and I will be their God, and they shall be my people. Wherefore come out from among them, and be ye separate, saith the Lord, and touch not the unclean thing; and I will receive you. 2 Corinthians 6:14-17.

These all died in faith, not having received the promises, but having seen them afar off, and were persuaded of them, and embraced them, and confessed that they were strangers and pilgrims on the earth. Hebrews 11:13.

Dearly beloved, I beseech you as strangers and pilgrims, abstain from fleshly lusts, which war against the soul. 1 Peter 2:11.

Ye adulterers and adulteresses, know ye not that the friendship of the world is enmity with God? whosoever therefore will be a friend of the world is the enemy of God. James 4:4.

Love not the world, neither the things that are in the world. If any man love the world, the love of the Father is not in him. For all that is in the world, the lust of the flesh, and the lust of the eyes, and pride of life, is not of the Father, but is of the world. And the world passeth away, and the lust thereof: but he that doeth the will of God abideth for ever. 1 John 2:15-17.

UNDERSTANDING THE SCRIPTURES

I have given them thy word; and the world hath hated them, because they are not of the world, even as I am not of the world. I pray not that thou shouldest take them out of the world, but that thou shouldest keep them from the evil. John 17:14, 15.

OBSERVATION #1: *The Scriptures consistently contrast that which is "of the world" with that which is "of the Father."*

Jesus was not "of the world." The "kernel," the "seed," the essential source of His life was from above. This distinction is not merely academic or theoretical. It found expression in all of Jesus' life from the words He spoke to the food He ate. It guided His decisions, His goals, His associations, His motives, and His actions. As a cluster of grapes is what it is altogether as a result of being "of the vine," and could not be a cluster of grapes if it had been "of a rock," so that which is "of the Father" will be of like character, and that which is "of the world" will be of an altogether different character.

All that is born of God, whether it be a person or the fruit in a person's life, will bear the character of God. It will have the life of God. It will have the righteousness of God. It will have the destiny of God. In contrast, all that is of the world, whether it be a person of the world or the things of the world or the fruit of the world in a person's life, will have the character of the world. It will have the stamp of the world's death on it. It will have the stamp of the world's nature on it. It will have the stamp of the world's destiny on it.

OBSERVATION #2: *Christians are IN the world, but not OF the world.*

Jesus did not pray the Father to take His disciples out of the world, but to keep them from the evil—literally, "evil one." So we are *in* but not *of.* All around us is that which is not of the Father; it is the domain of the evil one. The god of this world paints it with His colors, sprinkles it with his allurements, arranges it according to his purposes. We are in this very world, but when we are born from above, we are no longer of common stock with the world. We are of God— "And we KNOW that we are of God, and the whole world lieth in wickedness" (1 John 5:19).

OBSERVATION #3: To be kept from the evil [one] of the world, we must be "of the Father."

Father is a designation of God that only believers in Christ know. God has fathered them from above. Their life is His life. And as Father, He continues to bring forth His likeness in them by Parental care and training. Believers are "of the Father," then, not only in the initial sense of being born of Him, but in the ongoing sense of being reared by Him. They are "of Him" from beginning to end. In the hostile environment of the world, the believer finds his security in this initial and ongoing experience of being of the Father. The evil one controls that which is of the world, but he has no dominion over that which is of the Father. It is not his territory. "We know that whosoever is born of God sinneth not; but he that is begotten of God keepeth himself, and that wicked one toucheth him not" (1 John 5:18).

Study Questions

1. In what context did Jesus say these words? Does the time in Jesus' life add any weight to what He says here?

2. In what way was Jesus not "of the world"?

3. What does Jesus not pray for? What is His request?

39

4. In the Scripture, what stands in contrast to the expression "of the world"? Can you give examples? How does the principle "after his kind" apply here?

5. How can the concept "of the world" be applied in various ways other than in relation to people?

6. Describe as clearly as possible the nature of that which is "of the world." Describe as clearly as possible the nature of that which is "of the Father."

the fruits of the Spirit

7. Describe the implications of being in the world but not of the world. How will this concept affect our view of the world? How will it affect our view of ourselves?

8. How is being "of the Father" security for us? What

He expects → real lasting fruit

does the Father expect beyond our simply being born from above? What would be the effects of being born from above and being reared by the world? *We wouldn't really be changed.*

Be ye not unequally yoked together with unbelievers: for what fellowship hath righteousness with unrighteousness? and what communion hath light with darkness? And what concord hath Christ with Belial? or what part hath he that believeth with an infidel? And what agreement hath the temple of God with idols? for ye are the temple of the living God; as God hath said, I will dwell in them, and walk in them; and I will be their God, and they shall be my people. Wherefore come out from among them, and be ye separate, saith the Lord, and touch not the unclean thing; and I will receive you. 2 Corinthians 6:14-17.

OBSERVATION #4: *God calls us out of the world in order to bring us unto Himself.*

God's call is always directional. Every "out" has its "unto." Abraham was sent out of Haran to go unto "the land that I will show thee." The Israelites came out of Egypt to go unto the land of Canaan. And the believer is called out of the world so that God may bring him unto Himself. Unfortunately, many people are content with the "out" part of their calling. The Israelites simply wanted out of Egypt. They balked at the border of Canaan. But the terrible cost of refusing to accept God's "unto" is wandering and death in the wilderness. God's call is ultimately unto Himself, but there is no way to come unto the Father but by accepting His call out of the world.

OBSERVATION #5: *There is an irreconcilable opposition between Christ and the world.*

As we noted in the introduction, the difference between Christ and the world is a North Pole/South Pole difference. And just as the magnetic forces in the natural world generate opposite fields, so the opposing forces in the spiritual realm generate opposite forces. What fellowship? What communion? What concord? What part? What agreement? The answer to each question is the same, and it is unequivocal. NONE! The law of spiritual magnetism draws all things of God to God and repels all things of the world from God. He that would answer the call of God must come out of the world and be separate.

Notice, we are not even to "touch" the unclean thing. Jim Elliot, missionary to the Auca Indians, was so convicted by this truth that he prayed to be delivered from the desire to "fondle" the world. Some

Christians have released their grasp on the world, but continue to fondle it. They have left Sodom behind, but they continue to cherish it in their heart. They have sold out worldly goods, but they cling to the memories. Like the Israelites, they remember the leeks and the melons. "Touch not the unclean thing." Quit that fondling! That touch has an evil magnetism in it. It will take our eyes off the Father, set our hearts to discontent, and eventually draw us back to Egypt.

Study Questions

1. List the commands in this passage. How do the questions emphasize the commands? Make a chart showing the contrasts in this passage. Can you add to the list?

2. What does it mean to say that God's will is directional?

3. What is the danger of focusing only on the "out" part of our calling? What dangers are associated with focusing only on the "in" part?

4. Give some examples from Scripture of God's directional call. List more than those given here.

5. What promises does God give to those who separate themselves from the world?

6. What did Jim Elliot mean by "fondling" the things of the world? What are the effects of touching the world after separating ourselves from it?

7. What is meant by an unequal yoke?

> *These all died in faith, not having received the promises, but having seen them afar off, and were persuaded of them, and embraced them, and confessed that they were strangers and pilgrims on the earth.* Hebrews 11:13.
>
> *Dearly beloved, I beseech you as strangers and pilgrims, abstain from fleshly lusts, which war against the soul.* 1 Peter 2:11.

OBSERVATION #6: The call of God makes us strangers in this world.

Hebrews 11 chronicles the lives of many who heard the call of God and responded in faith. The call of God set their eyes and their hearts on things unseen—they saw a country not of this earth, they saw cities not builded by man, and they had a hope in things eternal. As they lived for that which was unseen, they became strangers to that which was seen. As by faith they laid hold of the world to come, they let go of this world. They became set apart, estranged from the things men and women of the world count dear. Like Moses, they counted "the reproach of Christ greater riches than the treasures in Egypt" (Hebrews 11:26).

Those who are strangers in this world are also pilgrims. The name *stranger* has to do with our present relationship; the name *pilgrim* has to do with our future destiny. We don't belong here, so we are strangers. We are going to that country where we do belong, so we are pilgrims. These two names again speak to the "out" and the "unto" of our calling. Because we are called out, we are strangers. Because we are called unto, we are pilgrims.

Study Questions

1. What is a stranger?

2. What is a pilgrim?

3. Who are some people who lived as strangers and pilgrims? What specifically in their lives demonstrated this?

4. What makes us strangers in this world?

5. How did Jesus live as a stranger? As a pilgrim?

6. How do "strangers" and "pilgrims" correspond to "out" and "unto"?

> *Ye adulterers and adulteresses, know ye not that the friendship of the world is enmity with God? whosoever therefore will be a friend of the world is the enemy of God.* James 4:4.

OBSERVATION #7: For the people of God to resort to friendship with the world amounts to spiritual treachery and betrayal equivalent to adultery.

We have noted that God's call is unto Himself. We are called into relationship. It is in that relationship that we have life. It is there we have security. Our relationship with God is not casual or incidental. It is radical and continual. Because the world is at enmity with God, we must renounce loyalty to the one in order to render loyalty to the other. The call of God is a call to covenant. He asks not that we consider following Him, but that we commit ourselves to Him.

Suppose a bride made this sort of "vow" to her husband. "John, I like you a lot, and I want to have the privilege and security of being your wife. I will come to live with you and I promise to give you most of my time and the biggest share of my loyalty. I should tell you, though, that I still like Bill a lot too. I would like the privilege of doing things with him at times after you and I are married. His Friday night parties are such fun, so I'd like to be able to spend at least one night a week with him."

God is no different in such a case than any sensible John would be. He would not count such a "vow" an expression of loyalty. The one night with Bill would render all the other nights with John a mockery. As it is on the marital level, so it is on the spiritual level. God asks for the kind of loyalty that is exclusive of others. Friendship with the world is spiritual treachery with God. We can understand, therefore, why God sets such a strict standard for marriage. Vow keeping is a matter of integrity. Where people are treacherous with their companions, they will be treacherous with God.

OBSERVATION #8: Allegiance to Christ resulting in estrangement from the world sets disciples of Jesus in a continual conflict.

In referring to believers as "strangers," Peter noted that fleshly lusts "war" against the soul. Within us are desires (lusts) that respond to the magnetic pull of the world. These lusts include selfish gratification, anger, immorality, covetousness, self-pity, and pride. Elsewhere we are told to crucify these desires. Alive, they war against the soul. They undermine spiritual vitality. They get in behind our battle lines and wreck havoc with the mind and will. Some Christians try to live for

God and pamper these lusts on occasion. The reasoning is that a little won't hurt. Feeding these desires in any amount, however, gives them the freedom to be alive and active. The death sentence is the only way to deal effectively with inner lusts.

Study Questions

1. What names does James use for those who are friends of the world?

2. What characterizes our relationship with God? What is our necessary relationship to the world in order to have relationship with God?

3. Why would a husband not accept a casual vow from his wife on their wedding day?

4. What is there in us that responds to the call of the world? How does this affect our inner life?

5. What are we to do with the desires within us that want to respond to the world's call? Find verses that tell us how to deal with these.

6. If we do not deal correctly with these desires, what will be the effects?

> *Love not the world, neither the things that are in the world. If any man love the world, the love of the Father is not in him. For all that is in the world, the lust of the flesh, and the lust of the eyes, and pride of life, is not of the Father, but is of the world. And the world passeth away, and the lust thereof: but he that doeth the will of God abideth for ever.* 1 John 2:15-17.

OBSERVATION #9: The "world" includes the whole system under the control of the prince of this world.

More specifically, it includes everything that pulls upon and preoccupies the physical, intellectual, emotional, and spiritual desires of people to distract them from God.

Lusts of the flesh: desire for food, desire for drink, desire for sex. What spicy foods the world offers to gratify those appetites! How the advertising world brings that food into focus!

Lusts of the eye: desire for properties, desire for vehicles, desire for clothes, desire for appliances and books and computers and machines and lawns and gardens and animals and tools and playthings and equipment and dishes and cameras and sound systems and collectibles and, and, and. . . . Again, the advertising media makes its appeal, holding its wares continually and provocatively before the eye.

Pride of life: desire for esteem; desire for notice and recognition; desire for a name; desire to have the honor of owning a company, accomplishing a dream, holding a degree, pursuing a career, leading a cause. The pride of life goes down to the roots of our being, down into the cavities of the soul. There at the heart of man is a place for God. It is a place of devotion. Man in his arrogance sets himself on the throne and looks to the world to satisfy the intense emptiness. When God is absent, everything in the heart of man amounts to nothing less than idolatry. Man's devotion was intended for God alone.

OBSERVATION #10: *Divine sentence upon this world system has been set—it will pass away.*

The devil is the god of this world. He is doomed. And when he falls, his kingdom will fall with him. All that is in the world, all that appeals to the flesh, to the eye, to the heart of man is only husk and shell, dust and ashes in the real sense. There is no enduring substance in the world. ALL will pass away. And all who feed on it are feeding on emptiness.

OBSERVATION #11: *The only safety from the destruction of this world is in God.*

King Solomon, frustrated at not finding meaning "under the sun," cried out, "Vanity of vanities! All is vanity!" Still, generation after generation tries to find meaning and purpose and security and happiness in the things they can feel and see. God doesn't intend that we find such things in this world. They just aren't there. God Himself is the ultimate meaning. His will is the ultimate purpose. Relationship with Him is the ultimate security, and knowing Him is the ultimate joy. God calls man to Himself, however, not only to meet man's needs but to rescue man from destruction. The judgment is set. This world will pass away. Those who do the will of God will abide—forever!

Study Questions

1. What are we told not to love?

2. What conclusion can be made regarding those who love the world?

3. What is the world?

4. List the three areas where the world exerts its pull on us. Describe each in your own words, and give specific examples.

5. How does the pride of life appeal to deeper levels of our being than the other two? In what ways does man attempt to replace God? What is the effect of being devoted to one's own ego rather than to God?

6. What will happen to this world? How does this show the folly of loving the things of this world?

7. What will happen to those who do the will of God?

8. How does Solomon's life emphasize the truth of this passage?

APPLYING THE SCRIPTURE

1. How have the "things" of this world multiplied in the past century, and what have been the effects?

2. Is the world growing worse; that is, is the Christian life becoming more difficult?

3. What are some of the major things in the world that are keeping young people from turning to God? What are some of the major things that trouble middle-aged people?

4. Consider each of the following areas of life that touch the world. What should be the Christian's view of these things? How does he determine what is right and what is wrong? What are some safeguards he can draw up for each area?
   a. Entertainment:
   b. Education:
   c. Business:

5. Is it possible to become entangled in "good" things to one's spiritual detriment? And if so, how do we avoid this?

6. Christians have often applied the "unequal yoke" to business and marriage relationships where a Christian is bound to an unbeliever.

   a. Name a number of business relationships that would illustrate this.

   b. Considering the context of these verses, the unequal yoke would have a much broader application. Any place a Christian attempts to mix the world with Christ, he is creating an unequal yoke. List some specific examples in the area of music, in education, in the home, in the church.

7. What are some characteristics of an alien (the literal meaning of stranger), and how can these be applied to the Christian?

8. What are some characteristics of a pilgrim, and how can they be applied to the Christian?

9. What are some ways Christians are being tricked into worldliness today?

10. What are some ways Christians can fortify themselves against the lusts of the flesh? Against the lust of the eye? Against the pride of life?

11. Are there ways Christians may think they are separated from the world and in reality they are very worldly? (For example, by avoiding the lusts of the flesh but indulging in the pride of life.) Be specific, but avoid venting personal bitterness if you have felt hurt by such people.

12. What frustrations have you experienced or seen in the lives of people trying to find meaning and happiness in the world?

PART II
UNDERSTANDING
COMMON PROBLEMS

"This know also, that in the last days perilous times shall come. For men shall be lovers of their own selves, covetous, boasters, proud, blasphemers, disobedient to parents, unthankful, unholy, without natural affection, trucebreakers, false accusers, incontinent, fierce, despisers of those that are good, traitors, heady, highminded, lovers of pleasures more than lovers of God; having a form of godliness, but denying the power thereof: from such turn away" (2 Timothy 3:1-5).

The predictions in this passage are being fulfilled in detail in Western culture. People are devoted to themselves, and self-centeredness is the seedbed of psychological, emotional, physical, and spiritual peril. Out of the press of a self-centered society come broken homes, abuse, rebellion, party-time values, much revelry, and a lot of frustration and heartache. People raised with the self-seeking mentality do not have a clear sense of reality. They don't understand themselves, much less the world around them. Values are upside down. Times are perilous.

Is there hope for believers in the end times? How do we cope with the pressures of our culture? In Lessons 4-9 we will study some of the common problems disciples of Jesus face in these end times. We will look not only at our problems, but at God's solutions.

Lesson 4

Self-Acceptance

INTRODUCTION

The subject we are about to look at is a delicate one. Many are the schools of thought on self-concepts today. Psychologists are fascinated with the subject. Ministers are interested. Fathers and mothers are concerned. And authors from all ranks are cranking out whole libraries of catchy ideas.

What is a proper view of oneself? Does the Bible have anything to say?

This lesson proceeds with the faith that the Bible does give us a proper view of ourselves, and that the Biblical view corrects misconceptions promoted by popular psychologists.

PERSONAL INVENTORY

1. In your thoughts, do you find yourself viewing yourself generally in positive ways or negative?

2. Do you repeatedly scold yourself for not doing better?

3. Are there things about yourself physically that you resent? (List them honestly.)

4. Are there things about your home life that you resent? Are there ways specifically in which you feel you were mistreated as a child or ways you were deprived of things that are important?

5. In a sentence or two write how you honestly think your parents view you.

6. Do you find yourself concerned about what people are thinking of you or what they are thinking of Christ?

7. Are you consciously desiring to have Christ live in you, to be changed in continuing ways to be like Him, so that in your interaction with others they see Christ in you?

8. Have you read any books on the subject of self-image? If so, what have been the lingering impressions you have had from the book(s)?

SCRIPTURAL BACKGROUND

So God created man in his own image, in the image of God created he him; male and female created he them. Genesis 1:27.

All have sinned, and come short of the glory of God. Romans 3:23.

Having the understanding darkened, being alienated from the life of God through the ignorance that is in them, because of the blindness of their heart. Ephesians 4:18.

The heart is deceitful above all things, and desperately wicked: who can know it? Jeremiah 17:9.

For I say, through the grace given unto me, to

every man that is among you, not to think of himself more highly than he ought to think; but to think soberly, according as God hath dealt to every man the measure of faith. Romans 12:3.

God is light, and in him is no darkness at all. If we say that we have no sin, we deceive ourselves, and the truth is not in us. 1 John 1:5, 8.

I am come that they might have life, and that they might have it more abundantly. John 10:10.

Abide in me, and I in you. . . . for without me ye can do nothing. John 15:4, 5.

He that hath the Son hath life; and he that hath not the Son of God hath not life. 1 John 5:12.

Not that we are sufficient of ourselves to think any thing as of ourselves; but our sufficiency is of God. 2 Corinthians 3:5.

I will praise thee; for I am fearfully and wonderfully made: marvelous are thy works; and that my soul knoweth right well. My substance was not hid from thee, when I was made in secret, and curiously wrought in the lowest parts of the earth. Thine eyes did see my substance, yet being unperfect; and in thy book all my members were written, which in continuance were fashioned, when as yet there was none of them. Psalm 139:14-16.

No man ever yet hated his own flesh; but nourisheth and cherisheth it, even as the Lord the church. Ephesians 5:29.

Thou shalt love thy neighbour as thyself. Matthew 22:39.

UNDERSTANDING THE SCRIPTURES

So God created man in his own image, in the image of God created he him; male and female created he them. Genesis 1:27.

OBSERVATION #1: Man was created in the image of God.

When God made man, man had a likeness to God that the rest of Creation did not have. Being made in God's image does not mean man is exactly like God. But man resembles God. The resemblance, likeness, image of God in man, apparently was intended to result in man bringing honor and glory to God. The image of God was not physical, for God is spirit, but man has a likeness to God in that he has personality, he has a mind, he has reason, he has the powers of choice, perception, volition, feeling, and appreciation. Man also has a spirit, "the candle of the Lord" (Proverbs 20:27). Because of this image of God in man, man was able to communicate and interact with God in ways the rest of Creation was not able.

Study Questions

1. Read the context of Genesis 1:27. What additional thoughts do you gather?

2. What does it mean to be made in God's image?

3. Does the dominion of man (v. 26) tell us anything about man being made in God's image?

4. What does 1 Thessalonians 5:23 reveal about how we are made?

5. Using word study helps, write a definition for each of the following:

   a. spirit   b. soul   c. body

6. What is meant in Proverbs 20:27, man's spirit is the candle of the Lord?

7. How does man communicate with God? (Study John 4:23, 24.)

All have sinned, and come short of the glory of God. Romans 3:23.

Having the understanding darkened, being alienated from the life of God through the ignorance that is in them, because of the blindness of their heart. Ephesians 4:18.

OBSERVATION #2: In the Fall, the image of God in man was marred by sin.

In his fallen state, man no longer bears the image of God as he did in Creation. Man's spirit died. His mind was darkened. His will came under the bondage of sin. All of his faculties have been tainted by sin—twisted and bent away from devotion to God, and given over to his own control. And so, by his sin, man fell from the place of bringing glory to God. Marred by sin, man became a shame and a disgrace.

Any understanding of man that fails to take this truth into account is riddled with error. Many today believe man is inherently good (in direct contradiction to this Biblical truth). Many believe that man has hidden potential and needs only to be taught how to bring it out. Seminars and books are offered to develop this hidden potential. It is true, man does have potential. It is true that training can develop hidden talent. But developing a person's talent will not restore the image of God in man. A cultured sinner, a talented sinner, an educated sinner, a professional sinner, a prosperous sinner, a likeable sinner—these are all still sinners, fallen from God and spiritually dead.

Study Questions

1. What happened to each of the following in the Fall?

   a. man's spirit

   b. man's mind

   c. man's will

2. How has the Fall affected the image of God in man?

3. What are some of the effects of the Fall not discussed here? (See Genesis 3 and Romans 5.)

4. What are modern misconceptions about man that contradict Biblical truth?

5. List some other Scriptures that state the effects of the Fall.

6. What are some of the deceptive effects of developing man's "hidden potential"?

> *The heart is deceitful above all things, and desperately wicked: who can know it?* Jeremiah 17:9.
>
> *For I say, through the grace given unto me, to every man that is among you, not to think of himself more highly than he ought to think; but to think soberly, according as God hath dealt to every man the measure of faith.* Romans 12:3.

OBSERVATION #3: Because of sin, man is self-centered; and in that self-centeredness, he is often deceived about who he is and what is best for him.

The heart of man was made for God. It is the place of man's devotion, the seat of control, the throne room, as it were. When sin separated man from God, the heart became the center of rebellion. Man took over the controls—life became centered around pleasing him, accomplishing his goals, and satisfying his desires. Devotion was shifted from God to man himself.

The shift away from God plunged the heart of man into darkness. Man is still able to think, but only as a man, not as a God-illuminated man. He sees only what his natural eyes can see, hears only what his natural ears can hear, and reasons according to his natural powers only. In this darkened state, he believes he understands many things, but he understands only within the limitations of his own observation and reason.

In the darkness of a God-empty heart, man is deceived about many things, but foremost, he is deceived about himself. The natural tendency is to think more highly of himself than he ought to, because personal ego becomes very important when God is not on the throne. If self is not elevated and gratified according to expectation, the natural responses are anger or self-pity. A person's view of himself may be up if others speak well of him, or it may be down if they don't. Unfortunately, a self-oriented heart cannot even read the responses of others accurately. A person may think, for example, that his friends don't like him when really they do. Or he may believe people adore him, when really they can't stand him. The heart is *deceitful* above all things. *Naturally,* we will have distorted impressions about ourselves.

Distorted self-concepts make for miserable relationships. As people value a high view of themselves, they seek for those situations that bolster that self-view. They plan their life agenda, weigh the merits of life's situations, choose their friends, decide what is good for them and what is not, all according to themselves. When people don't know the truth about themselves, however, they don't know what is best for them. They often want exactly what they need least. And the things they need most, they despise.

Study Questions

1. What does the Bible mean when it uses the word *heart*? Can you find Scriptures that help you understand?

2. What examples can you find in the Scripture of people who demonstrated devotion to themselves rather than God? What were the results?

3. From Romans 1, how does persistence in sin affect the heart and mind of man?

4. How does 1 Corinthians 2:14 describe the plight of the natural man?

5. What is man's natural tendency in thinking about himself?

6. How do people typically respond when they think others do not hold them in proper esteem?

7. What does it mean to think "soberly" about oneself?

> *God is light, and in him is no darkness at all. If we say that we have no sin, we deceive ourselves, and the truth is not in us.* 1 John 1:5, 8.

OBSERVATION #4: Man can understand himself rightly only in proper relationship with God.

God is light. The darkened heart of man desperately needs the light of God in order to be delivered from deception about himself and about his sinful condition. In his arrogance, fallen man does not acknowledge his sin. He justifies it. He looks at his circumstances as reason for sin. He holds others responsible—"The woman whom thou gavest to be with me . . ." (Genesis 3:12). How man needs God! The only proper way to come into the light of God is in brokenness, acknowledging our sinfulness. Once the truth of our sinfulness is brought into the light and we confess it and find cleansing, the Lord has freedom to begin beaming His light on the many other misconceptions we have about ourselves. We take up a walk "in the light," a light that continues to reveal our hearts to us. The more we walk with God, the more we come to see our utter poverty and His surpassing glory. Indeed, the more accurately we see Him, the more accurately we see ourselves. And thus, the knowledge of God is the only mirror for accurate self-concepts.

Study Questions

1. How does John describe the moral character of God?

2. How is this different from the moral character of man?

3. To be honest with God, what is the truth about ourselves that we must confess?

4. Which precedes which: honesty with ourselves; honesty with God? Why is the order significant?

5. What are the results of not confessing our sin?

6. What will be the effect of walking with God in the light?

7. How did Adam reflect the typical response of man when confronted with sin?

I am come that they might have life, and that they might have it more abundantly. John 10:10.

Abide in me, and I in you. . . . for without me ye can do nothing. John 15:4, 5.

He that hath the Son hath life; and he that hath not the Son of God hath not life. 1 John 5:12.

Not that we are sufficient of ourselves to think any thing as of ourselves; but our sufficiency is of God. 2 Corinthians 3:5.

OBSERVATION #5: *A proper self-image can be maintained only in devotion to Christ.*

Many are the offers in our society for those with a poor self-image. Seminars, books, and video series abound to pinpoint the cause (usually something our parents did wrong) and help us understand the cure (usually some five-step strategy that takes only five minutes a day and has built self-esteem in countless men and women who have become executives and presidents in major business ventures). These self-help programs usually have a certain amount of truth in them—that's what makes them believable. But do they make people less self-oriented?

Self-image is a puzzling thing. The more we focus on it, the less effective we are in dealing with it. We can change it, make it more pleasant, make it more acceptable to others, even make it respectable, without making it Biblical. Actually, the Bible doesn't tell us how to build our self-image. It tells us to devote ourselves to Christ. In the process of calling us to Christ, the Bible is rather harsh with self. "If any man will come after me, let him deny himself" (Matthew 16:24). For Christ to become the center of our life, self must be dethroned. Then the important questions are not, "What do people think of me?" or "How do I view myself?" or "Do I have a healthy self-image?" Rather, we are concerned with questions such as, "Is Christ having His way in my life?" "Are others seeing Christ in me?" "What do my friends think of Jesus?" The self-focus is changed to a Christ-focus.

Does this mean Christians do not think about themselves? Certainly not. But it means we are no longer absorbed in ourselves. With a self-focus, we develop patterns of anger, irritation, bitterness, pride, self-pity, complaint, indulgence, and self-gratification. With

Christ as our focus, we develop patterns of forgiveness, patience, kindness, longsuffering, humility, thankfulness, discipline, and love. Our joys and sorrows are wrapped up in Christ, not ourselves. What people think about us is less important than what people think about Christ. Whether people approve of us is not as important as whether we are reflecting Christ to them.

Jesus wants to live His life in us. He wants to transform us from the inside out to be like Himself. This transformation process of becoming like Christ is the only standpoint from which it is safe for a Christian to view himself. "We all, with open face beholding as in a glass the glory of the Lord, are changed into the same image from glory to glory, even as by the Spirit of the Lord" (2 Corinthians 3:18). Looking into that mirror, we see ourselves as continually in need. We come to realize it is not such a bad thing to be needy—it is actually a healthy self-concept. (See Revelation 3:17.) Looking to Jesus we find One in whom to glory. We are free to be base, despised, and weak ourselves without frustration so that the glory in our lives is indeed the glory of Christ (1 Corinthians 1:26-29). Furthermore, by looking to Jesus, we learn that accomplishment in the spiritual realm is only by Christ's enablement. Jesus meant what He said: "Without me, ye can do NOTHING." When Jesus lives His life in us, we have the freedom to stand back from what we have done in obedience to Him and leave the results with Him. Our self-concepts do not fluctuate with the success or failure of our ventures. We have no ventures. We have only Christ, and our desire is simply to obey Him.

This should clarify the radical difference between the Biblical teaching on self-concepts and the teaching we hear in our culture. Any attempt to deal with poor self-concepts that does not deal with self and does not focus on Christ is inadequate. Ultimately such attempts become strategies to retain self-centeredness and still find meaning, happiness, and fulfillment in life. We must conclude that counselors who offer green pastures to clients without calling for renunciation of self and devotion to Christ are thieves and robbers.

Study Questions

1. What are typical approaches in our society to a poor self-image?

2. Why does a focus on one's self-concepts only complicate the problem?

3. What are some of the evidences of a self-focus?

4. What are the evidences of a Christ-focused life?

5. From what perspective is it safe to look at ourselves?

6. List three self-concepts that result from a focus on becoming like Christ.

7. From your own experience, list some proper self-concepts you have found by focusing on Christ.

8. How do the approaches of modern psychologists deceive people?

> *I will praise thee; for I am fearfully and wonderfully made: marvelous are thy works; and that my soul knoweth right well. My substance was not hid from thee, when I was made in secret, and curiously wrought in the lowest parts of the earth. Thine eyes did see my substance, yet being unperfect; and in thy book all my members were written, which in continuance were fashioned, when as yet there was none of them.* Psalm 139:14-16.

OBSERVATION #6: Individuals are designed by God.

This concept is inescapable in the Scriptures, and its implications are weighty. God designed you. Physically, emotionally, and intellectually, you were made by Him. When we come to understand this important truth, we are in a position to accept ourselves. Many people today are under the bondage of resenting certain things about themselves. Their nose is too long, or their ears are too big, or they are too tall or too short, or they have the wrong color hair, or they are not smart, or they can't run fast, or they are too emotional.

This inner discontent is damaging in numerous ways. First, it accents a negative self-consciousness. Our thoughts about ourselves continually have the dark stain of resentment in them. The second thing discontentment about ourselves does, is that it robs us of gratitude. By focusing our attention on the one thing we dislike, we ignore many opportunities to be grateful. Notice the psalmist's attitude: "I will praise thee; for I am fearfully and wonderfully made." What a difference it makes in our attitude when we are grateful instead of resentful! The third result of being discontented is that we waste a lot of emotional and mental energy. Our negative attitude eats at our mind and spirit and saps our ability to think wisely and to have a bright outlook. The most damaging result of discontentment, however, is that it robs us of a healthy relationship with God. Since God is our Creator, when we resent ourselves, we ultimately are saying God didn't know what was best for us. We are believing that goals we have for ourselves are more important than God's goals for us. God knows all things. He knows what we will face in life. He knows how long we will live. He knows exactly what we need. Furthermore, God has a purpose for each life. And we can be assured that God designed us so that we would be best fitted to fulfill His purpose for us.

The question may be raised, "What about those with defects?" It is one thing, in other words, to accept being short or tall, but what about blindness? Does God design people with defects? Let's allow the Lord Himself to answer. "Who hath made man's mouth? or who maketh the dumb, or deaf, or the seeing, or the blind? have not I the LORD?" (Exodus 4:11).

Do we need to answer for God? Are not His power and grace such that He can use human weakness for His glory? Fanny Crosby, hymnwriter of the 1800s, was blinded at the age of two as a result of wrong medical treatment. She became one of the most influential people of her day. Hundreds of people came to her for spiritual help. Near the end of her life, her testimony was that blindness was one of the greatest blessings she had received from the Lord, and that if she had the choice to live her life again, she would choose it with blindness, not without.

Study Questions

1. What are typical things people resent about themselves?

2. Read the verses from Psalm 139 in several translations. What additional insights do you receive?

3. What is the psalmist's attitude about how he was made?

4. List four damaging effects of being discontented about how we are made. Can you list other effects?

5. List some examples from the Bible where God worked powerfully through human weakness.

6. Do more research on Fanny Crosby's life. How do you think her life would have been different had she been able to see?

7. Name specifically some things about yourself that you have struggled with wishing you were different. What does Psalm 139 teach you about what to do with these things?

8. Based on this study, write a paragraph describing a Biblical approach to self-acceptance.

No man ever yet hated his own flesh; but nourisheth and cherisheth it, even as the Lord the church. Ephesians 5:29.

Thou shalt love thy neighbour as thyself. Matthew 22:39.

OBSERVATION #7: *Self-love is natural; love for others is godly.*

We do not need to be taught to look out for our personal needs. We do that naturally. When we are hungry, we look for food. When we are cold, we look for shelter. When we are afraid, we look for protection. When we are lonely, we look for companionship. This is not necessarily bad; it is natural. When self is in control, however, this looking out for ourselves easily becomes selfishness. We go after food, shelter, protection, and companionship as well as any of our other needs with a primary view to ourselves, even at the expense of others.

In the natural man, selfishness may vary in degree. Some non-Christians learn a remarkable degree of unselfishness.

In Christ, we are called to love our neighbor as ourself. That is, we are called to consider his needs with the interest and concern that we naturally give to our own needs. This calls for love. Such love, John writes, is "of God" (1 John 4:7). God's love is extended to others, not because they deserve it, but because God is love. He views the needs of man (not always the same as their wants) and reaches out to meet those needs. He has been willing to do this even to the point of tremendous sacrifice (the death of His beloved Son).

Our love for others is to follow the pattern of God's love to us. We must not limit our love to the deserving, but extend it most to those who need it most. We must love out of the well of God's love in us. We must reach out with compassion even to the point of sacrifice. By such love, we demonstrate godliness.

The exercise of godly love is one of the best antidotes to poor self-concepts. Sometimes adverse home settings or broken marriages or misguided church settings can leave great scars on a person's life. Self-concepts take a tremendous beating. Failure and rejection are written all over one's life. If we do not learn Christ-centeredness, we easily grow bitter in such situations. One of the best therapies for battered, twisted feelings about ourselves is the exercise of love.

We must start with a renunciation of self and a devoted turning to Christ. Our number one objective must be to have Christ live His life in us. We then give ourselves to loving others. Instead of wallowing in our own troubles and being continually concerned with our needs being met, we learn to focus on meeting the needs of others. Such a focus is therapeutic. Love is healing. God's love flowing into us becomes God's love flowing out of us, and in the process our inner lives are restored. We learn that our worth is not in ourselves, but in Christ. Others come to value us for the One who lives in us. As Christ becomes our life, our self-concepts straighten out.

Study Questions

1. Look up the words *nourish* and *cherish*. How do they define our natural care of our needs?

2. List some needs we naturally look out for besides the ones listed here.

3. What are the marks of selfishness in meeting our needs?

4. What are the characteristics of God's love for us? List as many as you can.

5. How can these characteristics be applied to our love for others?

6. Why is it necessary to see love as being "of God"?

7. What limitations are we prone to place on our love to others?

8. What are some of the factors that commonly damage self-concepts?

9. How is the exercise of love related to the healing of poor self-concepts?

APPLYING THE SCRIPTURE

1. We are made in God's image. How should this realization affect the way we value people?

2. How is the philosophy of man's "hidden potential" being promoted today and what are the results?

3. This thinking (#2) undergirds many New Age beliefs and practices. To what extent is the church affected by these ideas, and how can we safeguard ourselves against them?

4. When man's heart is renewed by God, does he still struggle with a deceitful heart? Consider various Scriptures, such as Romans 12:2; Ephesians 1:17-19; 4:23; Colossians 3:10; and 2 Corinthians 4:4.

5. How do Christians get caught thinking of themselves more highly than they ought to think? What are the results of Christians becoming egocentric?

6. If it is true that man tends to think of himself too highly, why do so many people struggle with "low self-esteem"? (Note: Is low self-esteem simply the flip side of the same problem as high self-esteem? Are not both based on a high value of self—on the same self-orientation?)

71

7. What are some of the things people want for their self-image that actually are not healthy for them?

8. What are some of the miseries produced by self-centered living? When people learn tactics to deal with their resultant problems without dealing with their self-centeredness, what are the results?

9. What effects do we see in the church when people are still self-centered rather than Christ centered?

10. How does discontent with the way God made us find expression?

11. How can Christians help fellow Christians who are discontented with the way God made them?

12. What are some specific ways Christians can show love to the unlovely? What are some of the common ways they are tempted to limit their love?

13. What should a believer do when he wants to love someone but just doesn't feel able? How should he respond when he tries to love someone and his love is not received?

Lesson 5

Peer Pressure

INTRODUCTION

This lesson is closely related to the last lesson. Wherever peer pressure is strong, self-concepts come into focus.

Among young people peer pressure seems especially strong. And unfortunately, this strong peer pressure comes when young people are just beginning to grapple with their personal identity. The easiest way to handle the pressure is simply to conform to what others expect us to be. Conformity to peer pressure spares us the discomfort of being different and the tension of needing to explain why we are not like everyone else.

We are living in an age when social factors have increased the power of peer pressure. First, people are more mobile. Young people mingle with each other far more than they did a century ago. Second, technology has introduced powerful media such as TV, radio, video, movies, and on-line services which daily shape impressions and values both visually and aurally. Third, there has been a definite shift in the focus of society toward young people. The decibel level of young people, established in the 1960s, has never been turned down. Parents have been conditioned to listen to their children and accommodate their young people—to feel successful as parents, not when they have trained their children, but when they have developed strategies to live together with lower noise levels than their neighbors. A fourth contributor to increased peer pressure is result of the former three: insecurity. In a vacuum of enduring values, in a vacuum of healthy parental guidance, in a society where sex and fun and being cool are top priorities, young people are afraid to be different. The very things they run after undermine the kind of character needed to withstand negative peer pressure.

We can be grateful that the grace of God is sufficient for every human need. In this lesson we want to explore what is necessary to live for God faithfully, no matter what those around us might do.

PERSONAL INVENTORY

1. How would you rate the effect of peer pressure in your life?
   a. very strong   b. strong
   c. average   d. minimal

2. Can you list times when you have done something you didn't really want to do just because your friends did it?

3. Consider each of the following areas. Are there ways you have changed in the past year because of the influence of others?
   a. music   b. speech   c. clothing
   d. hairstyle   e. foods

4. In what ways have you observed your friends trying to fit into the "in group"?

5. Have you seen someone so controlled by the thinking of peers that you felt sorry for him?

6. What are some specific pressures you face from your peers?

SCRIPTURAL BACKGROUND

Thou shalt not follow a multitude to do evil. Exodus 23:2.

My son, if sinners entice thee, consent thou not. If they say, Come with us . . . Cast in thy lot among us; let us all have one purse: My son, walk not thou in the way with them; refrain thy foot from their path. . . . They lay wait for their own blood; they lurk privily for their own lives. Proverbs 1:10-18.

The fear of man bringeth a snare: but whoso putteth his trust in the LORD shall be safe. Proverbs 29:25.

For God hath not given us the spirit of fear; but of power, and of love, and of a sound mind. 2 Timothy 1:7.

For we dare not make ourselves of the number, or compare ourselves with some that commend themselves: but they measuring themselves by themselves, and comparing themselves among themselves, are not wise. 2 Corinthians 10:12.

Blessed is the man that walketh not in the counsel of the ungodly, nor standeth in the way of sinners, nor sitteth in the seat of the scornful. But his delight is in the law of the LORD; and in his law doth he meditate day and night. And he shall be like a tree planted by the rivers of water, that bringeth forth his fruit in his season; his leaf also shall not wither; and whatsoever he doeth shall prosper. Psalm 1:1-3.

But Daniel purposed in his heart that he would not defile himself with the portion of the king's meat, nor with the wine which he drank: therefore he requested of the prince of the eunuchs that he might not defile himself. Daniel 1:8.

UNDERSTANDING THE SCRIPTURES

Thou shalt not follow a multitude to do evil. Exodus 23:2.

OBSERVATION #1: The majority is not always right.

"Everybody else does! Why can't I?" Sound familiar? We use that line of reasoning to put pressure on authority figures to allow us to do certain things, go certain places, or wear certain clothes. That reasoning, however, ignores a more important question: Is it right? No matter how many people are doing something, we must be willing to ask what God wants us to do. If what others are doing is not right—if it goes against the Bible or if Jesus would not do it—we must not join them in doing it.

This principle is important not only in the world, but also among Christians. In fact, some of the greatest pressure to compromise comes from those who claim to be God's people. No matter how holy we consider the crowd, if what they are doing is not right, we must not follow.

OBSERVATION #2: *Group action creates pressure.*

This principle is not stated in this verse as much as it is implied. We are social people. We are concerned not only with what we do, but with what others are doing. Thus, we are much more affected by what the group does than by what one person does. What the "multitude" does, we want to do. Furthermore, the closer we identify with the group, the more pressure we feel to conform to them. Suppose among middle-aged people, it becomes popular to frequent a certain restaurant. An 18-year-old will likely be quite unaffected by a desire to go to that restaurant. He may not even be aware that it is "the" place to go for 40-year-olds. But if all his teenage friends regularly go to a certain eating place, he will be *very* aware of it and will be strongly motivated to go there too. Although consciously he may think of going there for certain food, subconsciously his motivation will be conformity to the group he identifies with—he is under peer pressure.

Peer pressure, in itself, is not necessarily wrong. God made us social beings, and He does not intend that we attempt to be individualistic just to avoid socializing. Acceptance in a group can be a healthy, cohesive force. We must be aware, however, of the dangers of blindly following a group. We must be guided and motivated by more than simply what others are doing. Doing right is more important than being accepted by our peers.

Study Questions

1. List some examples from the Bible where the majority was wrong.

2. What is wrong with the reasoning that we ought to be able to do something because others are?

3. What two guidelines are given above to determine what is right or wrong? Which is the more objective? List several more specific guidelines.

4. Why does the practice of Christians place more pressure on us than the practice of the world?

5. What are several factors that account for peer pressure?

6. In what way can peer pressure be healthy? After answering this question, try to define these terms:

   a. positive peer pressure

   b. negative peer pressure

7. Why is it important to be guided by more than a desire for acceptance in a group?

My son, if sinners entice thee, consent thou not. If they say, Come with us . . . Cast in thy lot among us; let us all have one purse: My son, walk not thou in the way with them; refrain thy foot from their path. . . . They lay wait for their own blood; they lurk privily for their own lives. Proverbs 1:10-18.

OBSERVATION #3: *Negative peer pressure offers many appeals.*

Sin is enticing. Satan sees to that. The enticement of sin adds to the pressure to be like others. There is always some purse, some gain, some apparent benefit to join in with the wrong crowd. Sometimes the reward offered is tangible—money, pleasure, or possessions. Usually, the appeal is deeper—acceptance, friendship, or prestige. The deeper the appeal, the more subtle it becomes. Many who can say no to money can't say no to an offer of friendship (or the threat of rejection).

What Satan and his crowd never show is what they take. Those who join the wrong crowd trade something for what they get. They may get money, pleasure, acceptance, and prestige, but at what price? Their integrity, their honor, their virginity, their honesty, their relationship with their parents, their relationship with God, their very souls. When we begin to deal on the black market of sin to gain acceptance, we are dealing with a master. Satan knows all the tricks of short-changing. With every little thing he offers us, he is sure to take far more.

> Still, as of old,
> Men by themselves are priced—
> For thirty pieces Judas sold
> Himself, not Christ.
>
> Hestor H. Cholmondeley

Study Questions

1. In Proverbs 1:10-18, what offers do the "sinners" make?

2. What are some of the underlying offers associated with peer pressure?

3. What valuable things do people often trade for acceptance with their peers?

4. What is the meaning of Proverbs 1:18? Can you list other Scriptures that state the same principle?

5. What does it mean to shortchange someone? How is Satan a master at this?

6. Study the account of Dinah in Genesis 34. How does peer pressure seem to have been a factor in her problems? What are some of the things she traded for acceptance with the "daughters of the land"?

> *The fear of man bringeth a snare: but whoso putteth his trust in the* Lord *shall be safe.* Proverbs 29:25.
>
> *For God hath not given us the spirit of fear; but of power, and of love, and of a sound mind.* 2 Timothy 1:7.

OBSERVATION #4: Fear of man will make us vulnerable to peer pressure.

Why do people cave in to peer pressure? Usually it is because they fear rejection from their peers. We don't like to appear odd. We are uncomfortable when we are different. These fears, unfortunately, are reinforced daily in our society by the advertising world. We are told to eat certain foods like Mister Celebrity. We are told to wear certain clothes, drive certain cars, use certain toothpaste, in order to be like Miss Celebrity. The

Mister and Miss always have bright shining teeth, full hair, perfect figures, and a glow of satisfaction that makes everyone want to be just like them. Since everyone else wants to be like them, we fear to be different.

Such fear brings a snare. We get caught doing things, saying things, wearing things, believing things that do not please God. We forget that that which is highly esteemed in the world is an abomination to God. (See Luke 16:15.) We find ourselves conforming to the expectations of others because down in our hearts we are afraid to do otherwise.

OBSERVATION #5: *By focusing on the Lord we can be delivered from the fear of man.*

"Whoso putteth his trust in the LORD shall be safe." Ultimately, it will not be people we will want our lives to please, but the Lord. When we bring the Lord into focus, our whole perspective changes. We realize how important it is to be approved by Him. We realize how small the evaluation of others really is in comparison. We realize, further, that life is short, that we are going swiftly toward eternity, and that choices we make along the way bear upon our destiny.

We must not only look to the Lord, we must also trust in Him. Making choices against the crowd may bring the disapproval of others. It may bring exactly what we tend to fear—rejection. That is why we need to trust. The Lord is able to carry us through such times. History abounds with examples of people who were not only rejected but despised and cast out, and who in that very rejection found greater joy in the Lord. The Lord gives His children His Spirit, and His Spirit brings to them His power, His love, and His sound wisdom. By focusing on the Lord, we tap into a strength that is far beyond our own. We are given the strength to love. We are able to keep things in right perspective, including the pressure of our peers.

Study Questions

1. What generally causes people to buckle to peer pressure?

2. Why is peer pressure such a powerful force in young people?

3. What are ways in which fear of rejection is reinforced in our society?

4. From the introduction to this lesson, list four social factors that contribute to peer pressure. Do you agree that these are increasing peer pressure in our society? Do you see other factors?

5. How is fear of man like a snare?

6. How does the nature of the world's values increase vulnerability to the fear of man? In other words, would the fear of not conforming be the same in a society that valued bravery and honesty, rather than such things as cars and clothes?

7. What specifically do people fear if they do not conform to peer pressure?

8. How do we overcome the fear of man?

9. How does the Lord change our perspective?

10. How does the Spirit of God stand in contrast to the spirit of fear?

11. How are each of the following important in withstanding negative peer pressure?
    a. power   b. love   c. a sound mind

> *For we dare not make ourselves of the number, or compare ourselves with some that commend themselves: but they measuring themselves by themselves, and comparing themselves among themselves, are not wise.* 2 Corinthians 10:12.

OBSERVATION #6: *Continually using others as our measuring stick is not wise.*

The dangers of comparative thinking are many. Measuring ourselves by others, we easily lose sight of God. We begin to feel smug about ourselves because we usually see others who are "beneath us." That leads naturally and swiftly to counting others as having less value than ourselves. This was exactly the problem at Corinth in relation to the Apostle Paul. There were apparently some who, not wanting to be under his apostolic authority, were comparing him with other apostles. We don't know what all the comparisons were that they were using, but we do know the effect—they looked down on Paul. And looking down on him, they were ready to cast aside what he said and operate the church by their own ideas. This second letter to the Corinthians is primarily an address to this problem and the confusion it was bringing.

While peer pressure is not in focus in this passage, we know that peer pressure operates to a certain extent on comparative thinking—being like others. The "in group" is not concerned with being like Jesus, but with being current with the latest fads in clothing and hairstyles, using the newest buzzwords, and having the latest hit albums and tapes. The effects of continually measuring ourselves by others are the same for us as they were for the Corinthians—feeling smug in ourselves and looking down our noses at those who do not fit into our group.

Comparative thinking is not wise! It clouds real issues. It distorts perspective. It is counter to the God-focused wisdom necessary for godly living.

Study Questions

1. Why were the Corinthians thinking comparatively about people?

2. What were the negative results?

3. In what way does peer pressure rely on comparative thinking?

4. What are some typical areas where young people face peer pressure?

5. In a typical "in group," where is the focus?

6. What are the effects of having these "in groups"?

> *Blessed is the man that walketh not in the counsel of the ungodly, nor standeth in the way of sinners, nor sitteth in the seat of the scornful. But his delight is in the law of the LORD; and in his law doth he meditate day and night. And he shall be like a tree planted by the rivers of water, that bringeth forth his fruit in his season; his leaf also shall not wither; and whatsoever he doeth shall prosper.* Psalm 1:1-3.

OBSERVATION #7: Because of peer pressure, it is important to avoid companionable relationships with groups of unbelievers.

Christians are in the world. They will relate to unbelievers. Indeed, they must relate to unbelievers if they are to evangelize effectively. But companionable relationships with unbelievers, particularly with groups of unbelievers, will undermine spiritual resolve. Notice the verbs in verse 1—walketh, standeth, sitteth. These verbs indicate companionship. Where groups of unbelievers are gathered to do what they want to do is *not* a healthy place for the believer to mingle. Blessed is the person who avoids such associations. Evil group pressure is difficult to withstand as an individual. Note also the progression of the verbs—walketh, standeth, sitteth. Association with groups of unbelievers may begin on the go, but it progresses to standing around, and finally to a comfortable sitting down together. Going a little with the wrong crowd ends up with joining the wrong crowd.

OBSERVATION #8: Safety against negative peer pressure is found in knowing and following God's will.

"His delight is in the law of the Lord." Simply staying away from the wrong crowd is not enough. If we are going to avoid negative peer pressure, we must have a clear sense of purpose in life. God's Word provides us with that. It shows us what is right, what is pleasing to God, and what is wise. As we become wise in God's ways by meditating on them regularly, we have a basis for evaluating group activity and group values. We will be able to discern whether it is wise to do what others are doing. When winds begin to blow that are contrary to our life's purpose, contrary to God's will, contrary to what is best for us, we will be like a tree. We will not be moved.

Many young Christians struggle with knowing how to have a meaningful time with God. The essential ingredients for a strong devotional time are found in Psalm 1. Notice the word *delight* in verse 2. Any devotional exercise must spring from a heartfelt and continual devotion to God. Notice also the emphasis on God's Word and the call to *meditate* in it. Devotional time must be centered around the Word of God—reading it, studying it, thinking upon it, allowing it to soak into the heart and mind. And finally, note the reference to "day and night." Our alone time with God must be inseparably joined to all of life. What we hear in the closet must form the framework for all our speech, attitudes, plans, and decisions outside of the closet.

He who delights in God and God's Word will want friends, but he will want friends who encourage his spiritual interests. Furthermore, he will value being right with God above being accepted by his peers.

Study Questions

1. Study the three expressions in Psalm 1:1. Then in your own words, try to state what is meant by each one.

   a. counsel of the ungodly   b. way of sinners

   c. seat of the scornful

2. Tell the difference between a Christian relating properly to unbelievers and a Christian mingling companionably with groups of unbelievers.

3. What are specific ways Christians may be tempted to mingle companionably with unbelievers?

4. What is the significance in the progression of the verbs in verse 1?

5. What is the safeguard against yielding to negative peer pressure?

6. What does it mean to "delight in the law of the Lord"?

7. What would be the effects of trying to avoid negative peer pressure without delighting in the law of the Lord?

8. How does God's Word equip us to stand against negative peer pressure?

9. In Psalm 1:4, how are the ungodly described? How is this different from the description of the godly in verse 3, and what analogies can we make about the differences in character?

> *But Daniel purposed in his heart that he would not defile himself with the portion of the king's meat, nor with the wine which he drank: therefore he requested of the prince of the eunuchs that he might not defile himself.*
> Daniel 1:8.

OBSERVATION #9: Withstanding negative peer pressure requires a heart commitment.

Daniel was not the only Jew in Babylon. Many choice Jewish young people had been deported from Jerusalem. They were all being sent through a three-year training program that was to equip them for service to the king. We can be sure Daniel was not the only one who was given food and drink that violated Jewish law. The compromises of his friends must have increased the pressure on Daniel just to go along with the Babylonian standards of eating and drinking.

"But Daniel purposed in his heart. . . ." Daniel's resolve is a living example of what we just studied in Psalm 1. He was like a tree planted by the river. He knew the law of God. He had apparently followed that law up to the time of this crisis. Now he was equipped to stand. Daniel's stand rose from a heart commitment. There was an inner yieldedness to the Lord, a commitment to follow God in spite of his setting, and a resolve to accept any consequences. Daniel was faithful because his heart was fixed.

OBSERVATION #10: By standing for God in the face of negative peer pressure, we make it easier for others to stand.

We read that Daniel purposed in his heart not to defile himself, but shortly after that we find that his three friends registered with him in the request to eat vegetables (v. 11). Daniel's resolve no doubt bolstered their resolve. Here we see the beauty of friends standing together. When a group does wrong, as most of the Jews apparently did, it increases pressure on all to do wrong; but when one stands up for the right, it gives others courage to stand also.

OBSERVATION #11: When we stand for God in spite of pressure to compromise, God works in our behalf.

"The eyes of the Lord run to and fro throughout the whole earth, to shew himself strong in the behalf of them whose heart is perfect [fully committed] toward him" (2 Chronicles 16:9). When we are willing to stand for the Lord, the Lord is willing to show Himself strong for us. Because of Daniel's commitment, he was no longer standing alone in Babylon. Nor were his three friends. The Lord stood with them. Throughout this incident and throughout the rest of the life of Daniel, we find the Lord arranging things for Daniel that Daniel never could have arranged himself. He served the rest of the kings of Babylon and then several Medo-Persian kings. It is nearly unheard of for a statesman of one kingdom to be set up as a statesman in the next kingdom. But because Daniel honored the Lord, the Lord arranged these details in Daniel's life. We read nothing about the other Jews. Those who yielded to the pressure of the Babylonian system became like the chaff. Daniel stood like a tree, and we continue to be inspired by the record of his life.

Study Questions

1. In what ways might the king's food and drink have violated Jewish law?

2. What indications of Babylonian idolatry do we have

    a. in the new names given to Daniel and his friends?

    b. in the kinds of "wisdom" used by the king's counselors?

    c. in the feast of Belshazzar (Chapter 5)? (Does this throw any light on the first question?)

3. What sort of men were chosen for this three-year training? (See the context.)

4. What did Daniel and his three friends have in common?

5. What is the significance of Daniel purposing "in his heart"?

6. When Daniel purposed not to do wrong, how did it affect his three friends?

7. What did Daniel do?

8. How might the example of the other Jews have influenced the prince of the eunuchs against granting Daniel's request?

9. List the things mentioned in Chapter 1 that God did in Daniel's behalf.

10. At the end of the training period, what were the test results? How does this verify Psalm 1? How does it verify 2 Chronicles 16:9?

11. List other examples from the Scripture of people who withstood negative peer pressure.

APPLYING THE SCRIPTURE

1. Make a list of ways you have faced negative peer pressure. Try to list them in order of significance.

2. Think of times you have compromised principle to fit in with a group. What were the issues? What might have been the results had you stood up for what was right?

3. In the introduction, four things were mentioned as factors for increased peer pressure among young people. Have these factors been evident in the church? Are there ways the church has contributed to the pressures young people face? What can be done about it?

4. How should church leaders respond to "in groups" among church youths? Should they respond to cliques among married people in the same way?

5. What are specific examples of negative peer pressure among Christian youths?

6. Psalm 1 teaches us to stand by delighting in God's Word. Many people struggle with meaningful devotional time. Why? What are rivals to a regular time of Bible study and prayer? What are ways to make this time more meaningful? Is there a balance between discipline and spontaneity? What are the effects of regular fellowship with God? What are the effects of not having regular fellowship with God?

7. In looking at Biblical examples of courage (like Daniel), what are more lessons we can learn for withstanding negative peer pressure?

8. Have you observed people withstanding negative peer pressure? How has their example inspired you?

9. Is it possible for positive peer pressure to work negatively? That is, do people sometimes do right only because others are doing so? Can this have its good side as well as a bad side? What might be the bad effects?

Lesson 6

Moral Purity

INTRODUCTION

"Ah sinful nation, a people laden with iniquity, a seed of evildoers, children that are corrupters: they have forsaken the LORD. . . . The whole head is sick, and the whole heart faint. From the sole of the foot even unto the head there is no soundness in it; but wounds, and bruises, and putrefying sores" (Isaiah 1:4-6).

Morals of North America? It certainly fits. Even if we don't have television, don't listen to the radio, and don't attend movies, we are faced with suggestion and temptation and perversion daily. Magazine covers in the grocery check-out line, pictures on the wrappings of simple household goods, advertising fliers in the mail—all these attack the moral purity of God's people daily. Those homes where radios and television and videos have free run are opening literal floodgates of immorality. The message is clear and it is brassy: "Sex is a number one priority."

God's people should never feel at home in the gates of Sodom. If we are going to survive the pressures of the world's immoral drumbeat, we must tune our hearts to a completely different wavelength. We must experience the cleansing of the blood of Jesus and the sanctifying work of His Holy Spirit. We must arm ourselves with truth, righteousness, and faith. And we must avoid the snares that Satan and the world continually lay before us.

PERSONAL INVENTORY

1. What is your relationship like with your parents?

2. What kind of music do you listen to?

3. Do you see any relationship between the above questions and moral purity? (Not necessarily your answers, but the questions themselves.)

4. How would you describe the moral temptations you have faced?
   a. overwhelming   b. very strong
   c. strong   d. mediocre

5. How badly do you want to live a morally pure life?

6. Are you prepared to be completely honest with God on this issue, including your past practices, your present mental framework, and your future goals?

SCRIPTURAL BACKGROUND

He goeth after her straightway, as an ox goeth to the slaughter, or as a fool to the correction of the stocks; till a dart strike through his liver; as a bird hasteth to the snare, and knoweth not that it is for his life. Hearken unto me now therefore, O ye children, and attend to the words of my mouth. Let not thine heart decline to her ways, go not astray in her paths. For she hath cast down many wounded: yea, many strong men have been slain by her. Her house is the way to hell, going down to the chambers of death. Proverbs 7:22-27.

And Amnon was so vexed, that he fell sick for his sister Tamar; for she was a virgin; and Amnon thought it hard for him to do any thing to her. . . . Howbeit he would not hearken unto her voice: but, being stronger than she, forced her, and lay with her. Then Amnon hated her exceedingly; so that the hatred wherewith he hated her was greater than the love wherewith he had loved her. 2 Samuel 13:2, 14, 15.

Ye have heard that it was said by them of old time, Thou shalt not commit adultery: But I say unto you, That whosoever looketh on a woman to lust after her hath committed adultery with her already in his heart. And if thy right eye offend thee, pluck it out, and cast it from thee: for it is profitable for thee that one of thy members should perish, and not that thy whole body should be cast into hell. And if thy right hand offend thee, cut it off, and cast it from thee: for it is profitable for thee that one of thy members should perish, and not that thy whole body should be cast into hell. Matthew 5:27-30.

Flee fornication. Every sin that a man doeth is without the body; but he that committeth fornication sinneth against his own body. What? know ye not that your body is the temple of the Holy Ghost which is in you, which ye have of God, and ye are not your own? For ye are bought with a price: therefore glorify God in your

body, and in your spirit, which are God's.
1 Corinthians 6:18-20.

For this is the will of God, even your sanctification, that ye should abstain from fornication: That every one of you should know how to possess his vessel in sanctification and honour; not in the lust of concupiscence, even as the Gentiles which know not God. 1 Thessalonians 4:3-5.

Purge me with hyssop, and I shall be clean: wash me, and I shall be whiter than snow. . . . Create in me a clean heart, O God; and renew a right spirit within me. Psalm 51:7, 10.

UNDERSTANDING THE SCRIPTURES

He goeth after her straightway, as an ox goeth to the slaughter, or as a fool to the correction of the stocks; till a dart strike through his liver; as a bird hasteth to the snare, and knoweth not that it is for his life. Hearken unto me now therefore, O ye children, and attend to the words of my mouth. Let not thine heart decline to her ways, go not astray in her paths. For she hath cast down many wounded: yea, many strong men have been slain by her. Her house is the way to hell, going down to the chambers of death. Proverbs 7:22-27.

OBSERVATION #1: Immorality is based on distortions.

Satan has probably gotten away with more lies in the area of "love" than in any other area. We will see this repeatedly in this lesson, but the above Scripture clearly demonstrates some of the distortions. The young man who is enticed by the woman believes he is in for a good time; instead, he is on a direct slide to death and hell.

Our world loves immorality. This means that our world loves to believe lies. Lies about immorality are regularly promoted in our society through songs, advertisements, movies, novels, magazines, and jokes. Following are some of the lies our society would like to believe:

a. That being immoral is better than living a pure life.

b. That a life of moral purity is boring.

c. That the more physically attractive a woman is to a man, the better.

d. That the ability to seduce a woman is a mark of manhood.

e. That sex will bring happiness and fulfillment.

f. That any given person's sexual drives are natural.

g. That consenting adults have the freedom to do as they please sexually.

h. That there will not be consequences for immorality.

These are Satan's lies. As Proverbs 7 demonstrates, men and women who commit immoral acts are deceived. Many strong men and many beautiful women have believed these lies and have been "cast down" by them. According to a government funded study done in 1991, the average American male has had seven sexual partners by the time he is forty. According to the Bible, we know that the more a life is filled with immorality, the more it is emptied of true joy and fulfillment. We can conclude that millions of Americans lead hollow lives.

Study Questions

1. The young man in Proverbs 7 thinks he is having a good time. List the figurative statements in these verses that are used to show the true picture.

2. Look back over Chapter 7. What tactics did the woman use to persuade the young man?

3. What is meant by the statement, "Many strong men have been slain by her"?

4. How do we know our society loves to believe lies?

5. How are Satan's lies about immorality promoted today?

6. Look at each of the lies listed above. Write a sentence for each one that states the truth.

7. What happens as a life is filled with immorality?

And Amnon was so vexed, that he fell sick for his sister Tamar; for she was a virgin; and Amnon thought it hard for him to do any thing to her. . . . Howbeit he would not hearken unto her voice: but, being stronger than she, forced her, and lay with her. Then Amnon hated her exceedingly; so that the hatred wherewith he hated her was greater than the love wherewith he had loved her.
2 Samuel 13:2, 14, 15.

OBSERVATION #2: What many people believe to be love is actually selfishness.

In this sad chapter of history, we see how distorted one's thinking can become when sexual passions are given free rein. According to verse 1, Amnon loved his half sister Tamar. As we read the account, we must conclude, however, that this was not the true picture. Amnon loved himself. He was so self-devoted that he was willing to defile a beautiful girl to satisfy his sexual desires. That is NOT love. It is stark selfishness.

Likewise many of the "love songs" of our day are not love songs at all but songs of selfish desire. It is lamentable that even many Christians cannot distinguish between selfishness and love. Love is a commitment to the well-being of another. It is self-sacrificing.

OBSERVATION #3: Infatuation (self-centered love) eventually turns bitter.

After Amnon had gratified himself, his feelings for Tamar did a 180-degree turnabout. Whereas before he had desired her beyond all reason, he afterward drove her out of the house. This is a sickening account of rape, but the principle is the same even when the infatuation is on both sides. The pattern has been repeated all too often since then—sticky infatuation turns to loathing. For a time, the very air is charged with love. No amount of reason can convince an infatuated lover otherwise. But when the sugar-coating of infatuation wears off, the selfishness underneath is revealed, and it is always bitter.

Even in Amnon's bitterness, however, we see distorted thinking. Earlier, he thought he loved Tamar— really, he loved himself. After his selfishness was gratified, the Bible says he hated Tamar. In reality, he must have hated himself as well. Self-gratification destroys self-respect. In sending Tamar out, Amnon was venting inner frustrations that are inevitable when people are self-centered.

Study Questions

1. What was Amnon's relationship to Tamar?

2. Why was he frustrated?

3. What kind of friend did he have? (See the context.)

4. What plan did they devise?

5. How do we know Amnon really did not love Tamar?

6. Based on this study, write a definition for each of the following:
   a. love   b. infatuation

7. What is the eventual outcome of infatuation?

8. How does self-gratification affect a person's view of himself? How did this find expression in Amnon's case?

> *Ye have heard that it was said by them of old time, Thou shalt not commit adultery: But I say unto you, That whosoever looketh on a woman to lust after her hath committed adultery with her already in his heart. And if thy right eye offend thee, pluck it out, and cast it from thee: for it is profitable for thee that one of thy members should perish, and not that thy whole body should be cast into hell. And if thy right hand offend thee, cut it off, and cast it from thee: for it is profitable for thee that one of thy members should perish, and not that thy whole body should be cast into hell.* Matthew 5:27-30.

OBSERVATION #4: Immorality begins with a problem in the mind.

Thoughts are the seedbed of action. Jesus cuts to the root of the matter in this teaching, showing that immorality is not simply a matter of action but also and foremost a matter of the heart. He who thinks immorally *is* immoral regardless of whether he commits adultery or not. Thus, the woman in Proverbs 7 was immoral in heart before she seduced the young man and in God's sight was guilty of immorality even if the young man would have said no to her advances. Furthermore, in God's sight, any man looking on who would have desired the woman for himself would have been as guilty as the young man who actually went in to her. We must conclude that flirting and lust are the first stages of immorality. Although a person may flirt or lust without actually committing fornication or adultery, the flirting and lusting reflect the heart of a fornicator or an adulterer.

What does it mean to "look on a woman to lust after her"? Does this refer to any suggestive thoughts that come into one's mind, or does it mean only those thoughts one continues to dwell on; and if it means the latter, how long can the thought be in one's mind until it becomes sin? We must beware of the tendency to deal with surface things and neglect root issues. What Jesus wants in us is a heart devoted to purity. It is not as important to establish whether a particular thought was wrong as it is to set our hearts on being pure. A pure heart is not above temptation, but it will struggle against sin, not relish it. It will seek out ways of fortifying itself against sin, not ways of indulging in it. When it notices the eyes looking at the wrong thing, it tells them to turn from it. Jesus' words are clear: to "look on a woman to lust after her" speaks of motive and intent. To use the eyes to feed one's lusts is immoral.

OBSERVATION #5: Whatever in our life causes us to stumble in this area should be "cut off."

Jesus referred specifically to the eye and the hand—both of which may be means of sin when the heart is immoral. Did He mean literally a person should cut off these physical members? Jesus has a way of putting things in eternal perspective. It would be *far better* to lose an eye or a hand (though they are vital members of our body) than to lose our soul for eternity. Better to go to heaven, in other words, with only one eye, or fully blind, for that matter, than to go to hell seeing with both eyes. Jesus is not prescribing literal action so much as highlighting the serious nature of sin.

We can make applications, however. Are there things that cause the eye and hand to sin? Cut them off! Are there books, magazines, novels, music, or pictures that would lead the mind into lust? If Jesus calls us to lay a vital body member under the knife's edge, how much more would He call for these channels of sin to be cut off? In the life of one who wants to live above sin, those things that lead to sin must go. There can be no halfway measures. There is no point putting in the closet something that belongs in the fire. Cut it off! Get rid of it! Burn it! Take care of it in such a way that you cannot go back and retrieve it.

OBSERVATION #6: *Sin has eternal consequences.*

In warning against immorality, Jesus spoke of eternal consequences. Sin leads to death. The end of lust is not adultery: it is hell fire. As One who understood *life* and *death* and *eternity* far better than a mere human, Jesus warns against the sin of immorality and calls to a life of purity. Immorality is not necessarily worse than other sins in this respect. Hatred and murder and stealing likewise lead to death. Immorality, however, seems to gain a special grip on the soul. Its bondage is strong as steel. Furthermore, when a culture degenerates, immorality seems to be at its worst in the final stages of that culture. Those who trifle with this sin play a deadly game.

Thank the Lord, there can be repentance. The power of Christ can break the bonds of immorality. The blood of Jesus can cleanse the heart of man.

Study Questions

1. How did Jesus raise a moral standard above that of the Law?

2. Where does adultery originate? Can a person commit adultery without having an adulterous

heart? Can a person have an adulterous heart without committing adultery?

3. What is the difference between an immoral thought and an immoral mind?

4. Why are people confused sometimes about whether a particular thought is sinful? How do Jesus' words clarify this matter?

5. How are Jesus' statements about cutting off body members to be understood? How do they help us to understand His teaching on this subject?

6. What are some ways immoral thoughts are fed? How should these things be dealt with?

7. In what way is immorality like any other sin? In what ways is it different?

8. What is one of the marks of a culture in its final stages of degeneration? What Biblical examples are there of this?

9. What breaks the power of sin?

Flee fornication. Every sin that a man doeth is without the body; but he that committeth fornication sinneth against his own body. What? know ye not that your body is the temple of the Holy Ghost which is in you, which ye have of God, and ye are not your own? For ye are bought with a price: therefore glorify God in your body, and in your spirit, which are God's. 1 Corinthians 6:18-20.

OBSERVATION #7: Christians should take special precautions against some sins.

The instruction regarding fornication is to *flee* from it. Does this indicate that other sins are not as bad? Not necessarily. But perhaps it recognizes that we are particularly vulnerable to this sin, and it is important to avoid it quickly and decisively. Some people could have drugs offered to them repeatedly, and their only response would be revulsion. It simply wouldn't tempt them. All Christians are wise, however, to recognize their vulnerability to sexual sins and take precautions against them. *Stay away* from places of temptation. *turn and run* from improper advances. No one can escape all temptation, but as Joseph's life demonstrates, there are times when the only proper route is *out.*

OBSERVATION #8: The Lord has set apart the body of a believer as a holy temple; therefore, sexual sins desecrate the temple of God.

In the Old Testament, God met His people in the temple. God's presence there sanctified the building and all its furnishings and utensils. To use the temple for unholy purposes desecrated the temple. Today, God lives in the hearts of believers. The body of a believer, therefore, is holy. We must not do anything with our body that would desecrate it as God's meeting place with us.

Sexual sins are sins in the body. As the context points out, fornication literally joins bodies—two become "one flesh." For a believer, this is a desecration of that which is holy. It is like trying to mix the temple of God with the temple of idols. What God has set apart for Himself He considers sacred. Even as the stones and wood and metals in the temple were no longer common stones and wood and metal, so the body of a believer is no longer just a body. It is God's temple. Keep it set apart for that which is holy!

Study Questions

1. How is fornication singled out as different from other sins?

2. What are we told to do in regard to fornication? What does this mean in actual experience?

3. What Biblical character exemplified this instruction?

4. Read Genesis 39:7-12. What progression do you see in Joseph's responses to this woman's advances?

5. What does 1 Corinthians 6:16 say about fornication? This demonstrates that a bond is formed. While this physical bond is not to be equated with the marriage bond, how does this concept further speak to the sin of fornication? How might a believer who commits fornication obligate himself in ways that hinder his freedom for the Lord?

6. Find Biblical examples of ways the temple (or its furnishings) was desecrated. What were the results? What does this teach us about our bodies?

> *For this is the will of God, even your sanctification, that ye should abstain from fornication: That every one of you should know how to possess his vessel in sanctification and honour; not in the lust of concupiscence, even as the Gentiles which know not God.* 1 Thessalonians 4:3-5.

OBSERVATION #9: Moral purity is God's will for YOU.

Having recognized some of the powerful ways the world exerts its influence on believers, having seen how vulnerable we are to sexual sin, and having observed the importance God places on the holiness of His temple, it is encouraging to know that God stands *for* our purity and *against* anything that would defile us. God wants us pure. He will work in our behalf within us. "For it is God which worketh in you both to will and to do of his good pleasure" (Philippians 2:13). He will also work in our behalf in the situations around us. "And we know that all things work together for good to them that love God, to them who are the called according to his purpose" (Romans 8:28). God is within us to give us pure desires and holy resolve. God is with us to keep us from falling. And God is around us to protect us from the enemy. "There hath no temptation taken you but such as is common to man: but God is faithful, who will not suffer you to be tempted above that ye are able; but will with the temptation also make a way to escape, that ye may be able to bear it" (1 Corinthians 10:13).

OBSERVATION #10: *Unrestrained sexual desires become unnatural.*

The "Gentiles," or unbelievers, walk in the "lust of concupiscence." We do not use the word concupiscence often nowadays. The Greek word here means "desire," and it is used in both a good and bad sense of desire and for desires other than sexual desires. But "lust of concupiscence" means "passion of desire" or "passionate lust." Those who feed their sexual desires in unrestrained ways, who gratify themselves in violation of God's commands and principles, easily turn normal sexual desires into ravening passions. Thus, the reasoning of some that human sexual desires are normal can be misleading. It is true that sexual desires are normal, but not everyone's sexual desires are normal, particularly when they have watched sensual movies, read romance novels, fed their minds on pornography, and practiced sexual sins for years. Our society is turning out people by the millions who believe their inflamed lusts are normal. They are *not*. The increase in rape, incest, live-in relationships, multiple partners, and cheating are indications that for many people, sexual desires are out of control. It is questionable whether anyone in our society with an average diet of movies, TV, and radio can reach adulthood with normal sexual desires.

Study Questions

1. Look up the word *sanctification* in the original language. How does this concept correspond to what we learned in 1 Corinthians 6?

2. Why is it comforting to know that moral purity is God's will for us?

3. What are ways God works in us? What are ways He works in the situations around us?

4. What is significant in 1 Corinthians 10:13 about the statement, "God is faithful"?

5. What is the meaning of the Greek word translated *concupiscence*? How is it used elsewhere in the New Testament?

6. What is the meaning of *lust of concupiscence*?

7. How is our society encouraging passionate desire?

8. How are people sometimes misled in thinking that their sexual desires are normal? What indications are in our society that sexual desires are not normal for many people? What Biblical examples do we have of communities where sexual desires had become abnormal?

> *Purge me with hyssop, and I shall be clean: wash me, and I shall be whiter than snow. . . . Create in me a clean heart, O God; and renew a right spirit within me.* Psalm 51:7, 10.

OBSERVATION #11: There is cleansing from sins of immorality.

David wrote Psalm 51 in penitence for the sins of adultery and murder. He had committed adultery with Bathsheba, killed her husband, and married her. But David repented. There is the crucial point—repentance. David's tears were genuine. He turned in sorrow *from* his sin *to* the Lord.

Notice David's emphasis on cleansing. Sins of immorality have a way of staining the heart. The conscience cries for purging. We may cover over the stain with ever so many excuses or activities or pretended happiness. We may try to smother the voice of conscience. But the reality remains. The stain is there.

Thank God for the blood of Jesus. "If we confess our sins, he is faithful and just to forgive us our sins, and to cleanse us from *all* unrighteousness" (1 John 1:9). Repentance is turning in sorrow from sin. Confession is naming that sin for what it is. When we repent, when we confess, when we lay out the heart as it is and ask for cleansing, *God forgives!*

The questions may come, How much detail do I name in confession? To whom do I confess my sins of immorality? Regarding details, the Scriptures reflect a balance that forbids vague evasion on the one hand and explicit description on the other. (See Proverbs 28:13 balanced with Ephesians 5:12.) Usually, more detail must be shared in private revelation or investigation of sin than is appropriate in subsequent confession(s). Regarding to whom confessions should be made, the general rule would be to all those who were wronged. David's confession (Psalm 51) shows clearly that all sin is against God, and therefore all confession of immorality must start with confession to God. David's sin, however, was also against Bathsheba, against Uriah, against David's family, and against the entire Israelite community (perhaps that is why his confession became a psalm for the entire nation).

The point of confession is to clear the conscience so that cleansing can take place. If we want a thorough cleansing, we must make a thorough confession.

OBSERVATION #12: *Cleansing from sin does not remove all the consequences of particular sins.*

Psalm 51 does not give us all the details. If we go back to the account in 2 Samuel 12, we learn that David suffered in several ways as a direct result of his sin. First, Bathsheba's baby died. Second, the Lord promised "the sword" (fighting and conflict) for David's future. David's own son later tried to take over the kingdom by force. Third, the Lord promised to raise up evil from David's own house. The next chapter records the rape of Tamar by Amnon, both of whom were David's children. And fourth, the Lord prophesied that David's wives would be violated publicly. When Absalom drove David out of Jerusalem, attempting to take over the kingdom, he spread a tent where all the Israelites could see and committed adultery with David's wives.

This principle is difficult for many to accept. If God forgives, why doesn't He remove the consequences as well? What we fail to realize is that sins of immorality touch many lives. When David sinned with Bathsheba, he brought reproach against the Lord. As Nathan put it, "By this deed thou hast given great occasion to the enemies of the LORD to blaspheme" (2 Samuel 12:14). David sinned against Bathsheba and her husband. As a leader, he sinned against the people of Israel. As a father and husband, he sinned against his own family. God could wipe away the sin in David's heart the moment David repented. But it was years before the reproach and disrespect were wiped away in the eyes of others (including his own children). "Whoso committeth adultery with a woman lacketh understanding: he that doeth it destroyeth his own soul. A wound and dishonour shall he get; and his reproach shall not be wiped away" (Proverbs 6:32, 33).

Study Questions

1. List the requests for cleansing in Psalm 51.

2. In which verse does David acknowledge his sin was above all against God? What words of Nathan may have been ringing in David's ears when he penned Psalm 51:4? (See 2 Samuel 12:14.)

3. Which verse in Psalm 51 describes the conditions necessary for being heard by God? What condition for cleansing is given in 1 John 1:9?

4. Why must we distinguish between sin and the consequences for sin?

5. What four consequences did David experience as a result of his sin?

6. List specifically the people who were affected by David's sin.

7. What tie do you find between the events in 2 Samuel 11 and those in 2 Samuel 13? We noted earlier, in other words, that Amnon lost self-respect through self-gratification. Who else had he lost respect for, and how may this have influenced both his inner feelings and his actions?

APPLYING THE SCRIPTURE

1. What evidences are there in our society that people have distorted ideas about love and sex?

2. How are distorted ideas about love and sex promoted in our society? Which ones have affected you most?

3. What distorted ideas seem most prevalent? Can you add to the list of lies given in the lesson?

4. Immoral thoughts lead quickly to bondage. We must not allow Satan any advantage. Are there any events from your past that have repeatedly come to your mind and tripped you up morally? Have you confessed them and asked for cleansing through Jesus' blood? Is there any particular area of your life—pornography, music, novels, joke books, videos, radio—through which you have repeatedly been ensnared? Have you gotten rid of all access to that area of downfall? (See Romans 13:14.) Have you fortified yourself through special prayer, Bible study, confession, and accountability schedules? Do you need an Ephesian bonfire? (See Acts 19:19.)

5. Read Isaiah 59:19. How may this verse be applied to our day? To a group? To an individual's life?

6. How can a person safeguard against the deception of infatuation? What part do our parents play in this? our church? our friends?

7. Study the setting for Amnon's sin against Tamar. To what extent is a good relationship with parents important for a morally pure life? (Study 1 Samuel 2:22-25.) Is there a tie between rebellion and immorality? What evidences are there in society for this tie? What does this tell us about submitting to authority? (See 2 Peter 2:10 for further study.)

8. How does the immorality of one person often affect many others? What does Jesus say in Matthew 18 about offending others, particularly little ones? How are many little ones in our society being offended? What will be the consequences? Note the progression in King David's

life from private sin to public sin—is that same progression evident in our society?

9. With immorality so prevalent, how can we "flee fornication"? How do we know when to stand and when to get out? Under what conditions might a Christian need to quit his job or move?

10. Confession of sin is an important step in cleansing and pulling down Satan's strongholds. What guidelines should a Christian observe in confessing sins of immorality? In other words, where is the place for clarity and the place for discretion?

11. In seeking God's cleansing and forgiveness for immorality, is it possible to be dragged too much into one's past? How does a person accept God's forgiveness? How does a person forgive himself? What are evidences of resenting the consequences of one's sins? What steps can be taken to overcome these problems?

Lesson 7

Submission

INTRODUCTION

Rock star, Alice Cooper, said this regarding rock music: "The whole idea behind the thing for me is rebellion. The worst thing in the world for me is that authority thing."[1]

In striking contrast, the testimony of Jesus Christ's teenage years was, "And he went down with them [his parents], and came to Nazareth, and was subject unto them. . . . And Jesus increased in wisdom and stature, and in favour with God and man" (Luke 2:51, 52).

While this lesson will focus on the importance of submission, we can hardly approach this subject without noting some of the chief strongholds of rebellion in our culture. Music is expressive of the soul, and it was no accident that rock music grew out of a subculture of protest. The music was designed to express certain themes—rebellion and sex, first; and later, the occult. Furthermore, it is no accident that forms of rock music continue to be major sources of conflict between youths and their parents.

The breakdown of authority in our society is huge, and it is far-reaching in its implications. We will not attempt to explore the whole social setting of modern American rebellion, but we are wise to be aware of it as we explore what the Bible says.

PERSONAL INVENTORY

1. What is your relationship like with your parents? Is it different now from what it has been in the past? If changes have occurred, what caused them? Are there any ways in which you are living contrary to your parents' counsel? If so, name the specific ways.

2. What is your relationship like with God? Are you close to Him? Do you sense that you are growing spiritually?

3. Have you had conflict with your parents over your music? If so, what have been specific things you have had conflict about—type of music? volume? amount of listening?

4. Have you dabbled in any way in the occult? If so, are you certain of complete deliverance?

5. What is your relationship like with your church leaders? Do you have the freedom to counsel with them? If not, what in your estimation are the reasons?

6. Are there any ways in which you knowingly and willingly violate civil laws—traffic laws, hunting laws, tax laws, etc.? If so, what are they specifically? What reasoning do you use for your practices?

SCRIPTURAL BACKGROUND

Let every soul be subject unto the higher powers. For there is no power but of God: the powers that be are ordained of God. Whosoever therefore resisteth the power, resisteth the ordinance of God: and they that resist shall receive to themselves damnation. Romans 13:1, 2.

Thou shalt not revile the gods, nor curse the ruler of thy people. Exodus 22:28.

And the man that will do presumptuously, and will not hearken unto the priest that standeth to minister there before the LORD thy God, or unto the judge, even that man shall die: and thou shalt put away the evil from Israel. And all the people shall hear, and fear, and do no more presumptuously. Deuteronomy 17:12, 13.

Honour thy father and thy mother: that thy days may be long upon the land which the LORD thy God giveth thee. He that curseth his father, or his mother, shall surely be put to death. Exodus 20:12; 21:17.

The eye that mocketh at his father, and despiseth to obey his mother, the ravens of the valley shall pick it out, and the young eagles shall eat it. Proverbs 30:17.

Hath the LORD as great delight in burnt offerings and sacrifices, as in obeying the voice of the LORD? Behold, to obey is better than sacrifice, and to hearken than the fat of rams. For rebellion is as the sin of witchcraft, and stubbornness is as iniquity and idolatry. 1 Samuel 15:22, 23.

The centurion answered and said, Lord, I am not worthy that thou shouldest come under my roof: but speak the word only, and my servant shall be healed. For I am a man under authority, having soldiers under me: and I say to this man, Go, and he goeth; and to another, Come, and he cometh; and to my servant, Do this, and he doeth it. When Jesus heard it, he marvelled, and said to them that followed, Verily I say unto you, I have not found so great faith, no, not in Israel. Matthew 8:8-10.

But I would have you know, that the head of every man is Christ; and the head of the woman is the man; and the head of Christ is God. 1 Corinthians 11:3.

Servants, be subject to your masters with all fear; not only to the good and gentle, but also to the froward. 1 Peter 2:18.

Remember them which have the rule over you, who have spoken unto you the word of God: whose faith follow, considering the end of their conversation. Obey them that have the rule over you, and submit yourselves: for they watch for your souls, as they that must give account, that they may do it with joy, and not with grief: for that is unprofitable for you. Hebrews 13:7, 17.

Likewise, ye younger, submit yourselves unto the elder. Yea, all of you be subject one to another, and be clothed with humility: for God resisteth the proud, and giveth grace to the humble. 1 Peter 5:5.

Then Peter and the other apostles answered and said, We ought to obey God rather than men. Acts 5:29.

This know also, that in the last days perilous times shall come. For men shall be lovers of their own selves . . . disobedient to parents. 2 Timothy 3:1, 2.

UNDERSTANDING THE SCRIPTURES

Let every soul be subject unto the higher powers. For there is no power but of God: the powers that be are ordained of God. Whosoever therefore resisteth the power, resisteth the ordinance of God: and they that resist shall receive to themselves damnation. Romans 13:1, 2.

Thou shalt not revile the gods, nor curse the ruler of thy people. Exodus 22:28.

And the man that will do presumptuously, and will not hearken unto the priest that standeth to minister there before the LORD thy God, or unto the judge, even that man shall die: and thou shalt put away the evil from Israel. And all the people shall hear, and fear, and do no more presumptuously. Deuteronomy 17:12, 13.

OBSERVATION #1: *All authority rests in God.*

These Scriptures are dealing with civil authority. We have all seen the flashing lights of a squad car, the soldier's uniform, the badge, the flag—symbols of a country's authority. These passages declare that all such authority is of God, and on that basis, we are to show respect and render obedience.

God is over all. He is the sovereign Lord—*God*, in the total sense of the word. There is no changing that reality. His power and rule are over all men, over all of Creation, over heaven and earth, for all time and eternity.

God has vested authority in man. He ordained civil rulership, as we see in Romans 13. He also ordained the home and the church with an order of authority. These lines of authority vary in purpose and in character. The home, the state, and the church each has a different function in our world; and the father, therefore, does not operate the same way a policeman does. But each authority has his proper place, his area of responsibility, and his mandates from God. And each of these lines of authority traces directly to God. For God is *over all*.

OBSERVATION #2: *Since God has given authority to men, to resist those in authority is equivalent to resisting God.*

Again, civil rulers are in focus in the above Scriptures, but the principle of resisting authority can be applied to all God-ordained authority. Because God stands at the head of all authority, resisting authority at any point means resisting God. Backtalk, disobedience, mockery, disrespect, refusal to accept decisions (whether from policemen, parents, husbands, ministers, or employers) is serious business in God's sight. It is breaking down that which God has set up. It is despising what He has ordained. To resist authority, therefore, is ultimately to set ourselves up for a meeting with God, because He stands behind those He delegates. "They that resist shall receive to themselves damnation."

Study Questions

1. In Romans 13 what is meant by the term "higher powers"?

2. List the things in this passage Christians are told to do. (Check on down through verse 8.)

3. List several expressions from Romans 13 that show the relationship of civil authority to God. What do these statements teach us?

4. Since God is the final authority, what are we doing when we resist human authority?

5. How are Exodus 22:28 and Acts 23:5 related? How are rulers commonly reviled today?

6. Study the context of Deuteronomy 17:12, 13. What situation is being described? What were the people to do with difficult cases? How were people to respond to the verdict of the judges? What was to happen if people disregarded the judge's orders?

7. What ultimately will happen to people who resist authority God has set up?

> *Honour thy father and thy mother: that thy days may be long upon the land which the* Lord *thy God giveth thee. He that curseth his father, or his mother, shall surely be put to death.* Exodus 20:12; 21:17.
>
> *The eye that mocketh at his father, and despiseth to obey his mother, the ravens of the valley shall pick it out, and the young eagles shall eat it.* Proverbs 30:17.

OBSERVATION #3: Respect for authority provides protection.

We may not understand all of God's reasons for establishing authority structures, but some reasons are more clear than others. Romans 13, for example, would teach us that order is one of God's purposes. When authority breaks down, order breaks down. Unfortunately, in our fallen state, we easily overlook another purpose for authority—protection. We tend to think that authority keeps us from what we want. The more we rebel, the more we resent restrictions. We feel inhibited. Authority stands in our way.

The prodigal son apparently felt that way, so he packed up his money and went out to do as he merry well pleased. He found that his father's authority had kept him for years from the fun of drinking parties and wild, immoral living. But eventually, he came to realize that his father's authority had also kept him from poverty, from loneliness, from heartache, from hunger and disease. When he came to himself, he suddenly understood the protection his father's authority had provided. And he reasoned it would be better to be a servant within the protective walls of his father's authority than to be a son outside of those walls. He was willing, in other words, to give his father even more authority over him than before.

The call to honor parents is "that it may be well with thee." God knows the dangers of independence and rebellion. In His sovereignty, He not only established authority but also ordained the consequences for resisting authority. It is only the deceitfulness of sin that causes us to resent being under those God has placed over us. God intended that we value authority, that we cherish being accountable, that we honor parents (and other authorities) for their role in keeping us from the heartache and grief of disobedience.

OBSERVATION #4: *The home is the foundation for learning submission.*

The first place anyone encounters authority is in the home. Much as babies are cuddled and waited on hand and foot during the first part of their lives, they eventually must learn to yield. Crying will not always get them their way. The things they want to explore are not always in their best interests. Their parents need to teach them that potting soil is not a good diet, that paring knives are not safe toys, that a hot cup of coffee is not a safe drink for them. Children balk. They don't understand. But they need to learn submission.

The early years of training largely determine the quality of submission later. It is relatively easy to control a small child without requiring submission. Place the plant, the knives, and the hot cup out of reach. When the child screams, turn your back and walk away; or get him to laugh and forget about what he wants. Such a child may be kept from doing something harmful, but he is not being taught submission. When a child is not taught to submit to a firm NO from his parents, he will have trouble accepting a firm NO from the teacher, from the state, from the employer, from the church, and from the Bible.

Study Questions

1. What reason is given in Exodus 20 for honoring one's parents? What consequence was there to be for cursing one's parents?

2. According to Proverbs 30:17, what are the consequences for not honoring one's parents? This is figurative language. How would you state the same idea in literal language?

3. What is a fairly clear purpose for authority? Can you name others?

4. How does authority provide protection?

5. What are some things the prodigal son apparently wanted? What are some things his father's authority protected him from that he wasn't aware of? What did he conclude in regard to his father's authority?

6. Why is it important to learn submission in the home?

7. What are some examples of toddlers wanting things that are not good for them?

8. How do older people sometimes keep young children from doing what is harmful without teaching them obedience? What are the results?

> *Hath the LORD as great delight in burnt offerings and sacrifices, as in obeying the voice of the LORD? Behold, to obey is better than sacrifice, and to hearken than the fat of rams. For rebellion is as the sin of witchcraft, and stubbornness is as iniquity and idolatry.* 1 Samuel 15:22, 23.

OBSERVATION #5: Rebellion indicates the working of Satan.

Satan is the author of rebellion. He set his heart on the throne of God and wanted to be like the Most High. And he has been busy in every generation of men to spread rebellion, to stir men and women to disobedience against the commands of God. In the setting of the above Scripture, Samuel was rebuking Saul for disobedience, and he declared, "Rebellion is as the sin of witchcraft, and stubbornness is as . . . idolatry!" When we take our own way, we are joining forces with the chief rebel against God's authority—Satan. Rebellion in the heart of man gives the devil access to carry on his program. Where people disregard authority, Satan has a heyday. Sins of all sort break out.

That is why rock music has had such an impact on our culture. It was music of protest, music that blatantly scoffed at rules and convention and authority. Under the spell of rock music, millions of teenagers threw off the authority of their parents, policemen, and pastors. Their rebellion led them into drugs, sex, and violence; and eventually, it led them into the occult. It is no accident that Satanic symbols and occult lyrics abound in certain kinds of music. The music is suited to the nature of Satan. Jim Steinman, from the rock group Meat Loaf, said, "There is no disputing that satanic and occult connections occur in the rock world." And Mick Jones of The Clash has added, "There's definitely some inner magic circle with rock 'n' roll. We've encountered it enough times to be certain of that."[2]

OBSERVATION #6: *A person with an independent spirit often attempts to camouflage rebellion and disobedience behind good motives.*

Samuel confronted Saul with the charge of disobedience. Saul responded by saying he HAD obeyed the Lord. And he had, partially. But that smoke screen of partial obedience was not enough to hide King Agag and the large herds of animals Saul had spared. Saul appealed to his motives—he had spared the animals for sacrifice to the Lord. He attempted to shift the blame to the people. But the Lord kept His finger pointed at Saul's disobedience until Saul finally acknowledged, "I have sinned." Unfortunately, Saul didn't repent and the direction of his life from that point on was downhill.

From Saul's life, we can see a number of characteristics of an independent spirit:

a. Ignoring or bypassing authority figures God has placed over me.

b. Desiring responsibility, but resenting accountability.

c. Rearranging commands to suit personal interests.

d. Using justification or blame-shifting tactics when confronted.

e. Giving commands, but refusing instruction.

f. Resisting God's reproofs for disobedience.

g. Being harsh with subordinates.

Study Questions

1. Read the story in 1 Samuel 15 that led up to the rebuke in verse 22. What was Saul told to do? What did Saul do? What was the Lord's word to Samuel? What were Saul's first words to Samuel?

2. Who is the author of rebellion?

3. Why is rebellion such an offense to God?

4. What happens when people rebel against authority?

5. Describe the ties between rock music and rebellion. Name some of the ways teenagers demonstrated their rebellion with the advent of rock music.

6. What connection is there between rock music and the occult? Consider the three quotations from rock musicians themselves regarding their music. (Alice Cooper's is given in the introduction). What conclusions can we draw?

7. What were the excuses Saul gave for disobeying the Lord? How do we know Saul did not repent, though he acknowledged his sin?

8. From Saul's life, find the incident or list the verse where he demonstrated each of the marks of an independent spirit.

9. Write out seven marks of a submissive spirit in contrast to the seven marks of an independent spirit.

> *The centurion answered and said, Lord, I am not worthy that thou shouldest come under my roof: but speak the word only, and my servant shall be healed. For I am a man under authority, having soldiers under me: and I say to this man, Go, and he goeth; and to another, Come, and he cometh; and to my servant, Do this, and he doeth it. When Jesus heard it, he marvelled, and said to them that followed, Verily I say unto you, I have not found so great faith, no, not in Israel.* Matthew 8:8-10.

OBSERVATION #7: *A person's effectiveness in exercising authority depends much on how faithfully he honors authority.*

The centurion understood an important concept about his position—he was under Roman authority. Most people view such a position as "having authority" rather than being "under authority." The centurion realized, however, that when he gave commands to his servants, those commands were to be in harmony with Roman rule. And when they were, all Roman power was behind the commands. Faithfulness "under authority" gave the centurion perfect freedom to exercise his authority as a centurion.

He applied this concept to Jesus. Jesus, he believed, had the authority to heal. He had it by being perfectly under the authority of God. For Jesus to say to sickness, "Depart," was no more difficult than for the centurion to say to a servant, "Go." The centurion felt unworthy to have Jesus come into his house, so he simply asked Jesus to exercise His authority the way a centurion would. Just as "all Rome" was behind the centurion's commands, so "all heaven" was behind Jesus' commands.

Jesus commended the centurion for his faith—his simple belief in the authority of Jesus. And He healed the centurion's servant with only a spoken command. Jesus' authority, like the centurion's, stemmed from being perfectly under authority.

Study Questions

1. What was the centurion's problem? (See the context.)

2. What did he request of Jesus?

3. Why didn't he want Jesus to come to his house?

4. How did the centurion describe himself? How did he use himself as an illustration of Jesus' authority?

5. Why did Jesus marvel? How did the centurion's reasoning demonstrate faith?

6. In your own words describe the authority concepts of the centurion.

7. Using a concordance, find places where Jesus stated that His work on earth was altogether a matter of obeying His Father—He said only what He was told to say and did only what He was told to do. (The Gospel of John contains numerous such statements.) What can we learn from this, especially as we consider the authority principles stated by the centurion?

But I would have you to know, that the head of every man is Christ; and the head of the woman is the man; and the head of Christ is God. 1 Corinthians 11:3.

Servants, be subject to your masters with all fear; not only to the good and gentle, but also to the froward. 1 Peter 2:18.

Remember them which have the rule over you, who have spoken unto you the word of God: whose faith follow, considering the end of their conversation. Obey them that have the rule over you, and submit yourselves: for they watch for your souls, as they that must give account, that they may do it with joy, and not with grief: for that is unprofitable for you. Hebrews 13:7, 17.

> *Likewise, ye younger, submit yourselves unto the elder. Yea, all of you be subject one to another, and be clothed with humility: for God resisteth the proud, and giveth grace to the humble.* 1 Peter 5:5.

OBSERVATION #8: Submission is a virtue to be exercised in a variety of relationships. NO ONE is excluded from the obligation to submit.

Every person is under authority. The man, the woman, the worker, the civilian, the church member, and the pastor—all must learn to submit. Learning to honor those in authority:

a. Opens us to the Lord's grace.

b. Spares us from God's reproofs for disobedience and rebellion.

c. Protects us from our spiritual enemy, Satan.

d. Yields joy in authority relationships, rather than tension.

e. Opens our lives to wisdom through counsel from authority figures.

f. Develops other qualities of character that accompany humility.

g. Makes us teachable and cooperative in our spirit.

h. Spares us from responsibilities we are not intended to carry.

i. Gives us a solid premise for saying no to wrongdoing.

j. Makes our life an example to others.

When we understand these blessings of submission, we will seek to honor those God has placed over us. We will avoid situations where we are "on our own" but, rather, will make ourselves accountable.

Study Questions

1. Describe the order of authority in the home.

2. What principles guide employees in relating to their employers? (See also Ephesians 6:5-8.) What is a "froward" person? (Check a different translation.) What are some ways an employer can be "froward"? What are possible responses of a Christian employee in such situations?

3. List the obligations of church members to their leaders as stated in Hebrews 13:7, 17. Include also what is given in 1 Thessalonians 5:12, 13.

4. What will church leaders need to do at the end of their ministry? How should this affect the way we relate to them?

5. What quality is necessary for submitting one to another?

6. What is God's relationship to the proud?

7. Looking at the list of blessings for honoring those in authority, which are particularly striking to you? Make a list that would show the contrast. In other words, if we do not honor authority figures, what will be the results?

8. How can we sometimes place ourselves under authority even when we are "on our own"?

> *Then Peter and the other apostles answered and said, We ought to obey God rather than men.* Acts 5:29.

OBSERVATION #9: Since God is the ultimate authority, when human authority commands what God forbids, or forbids what God commands, we must obey God rather than man.

In this setting, the apostles had been commanded not to speak or teach in the name of Jesus. This was in direct contradiction to the commission Jesus had given them to be witnesses in Jerusalem, in Judea, in Samaria, and unto the whole world. The disciples were not being rebellious. They were not defiant in their spirit. Notice their wording: "We ought to obey. . . . Their emphasis was on being obedient—they simply realized that in this conflict they needed to render their obedience to God rather than to man.

When human authority and God's authority clash, the spirit of those under authority is very important. Their bearing, their words, their attitudes, their actions, all testify whether in spirit they are submissive or defiant. God's people should never raise the clenched fist in the face of authority figures who are out of place. They must have the strength of meekness, the inner power that is willing to stand, but not to retaliate; for those who obey God rather than man may need to suffer for their faith. And as Peter wrote later, Christians ought not to suffer for wrongdoing, "but if, when ye do well, and suffer for it, ye take it patiently, this is acceptable with God" (1 Peter 2:20).

When conflict arises between what man says and

what God says, sometimes an appeal can avert a confrontation. Daniel purposed not to defile himself with the king's meat, but rather than bringing the issue to immediate confrontation with a "No way!" he appealed to the officer over the eunuchs, offering an alternative that was acceptable to his conscience. In that account, we find that Daniel's manner had already won him a hearing with his authority. The prince of the eunuchs knew Daniel was not being obstinate, and he did what he could to accommodate Daniel's request.

Study Questions

1. From Acts 4, find the order the Jewish leaders gave the apostles. Write a command of Jesus that this order opposed. Find a verse in Acts 4 that states essentially the statement the apostles made in Acts 5:29.

2. What about the wording indicates that the disciples were not rebelling in heart in going against the order of the Jewish leaders?

3. In a situation such as the disciples were in, how might a person demonstrate a wrong attitude? What would be the results?

4. Describe the proper attitude of a person who must go against human authority in obeying God.

5. When a person obeys God rather than man, what must he be willing to do? How did the disciples respond to their suffering in this case? (See Acts 5:41.)

6. What is one way to avert a confrontation when there is conflict in authority? How does Daniel's example give us guidelines for making an appeal?

> *This know also, that in the last days per-ilous times shall come. For men shall be lovers of their own selves . . . disobedient to parents.* 2 Timothy 3:1, 2.

OBSERVATION #10: *The breakdown of author-ity is a danger signal in a culture.*

We have already noted some of the indications in our society of a breakdown in authority. As someone has noted in public schools, teachers are afraid of the school board, the school board is afraid of the parents, the parents are afraid of their children, and the children are afraid of nobody. The degeneration of author-ity is evident in public education as much as anywhere. The following comparison demonstrates the deteriora-tion. These are the seven top problems in public schools in 1940 as compared to 40 years later in 1980:

1940	1980
1. Talking	1. Drug abuse
2. Chewing gum	2. Alcohol abuse
3. Making noise	3. Pregnancy
4. Running in the hall	4. Suicide
5. Getting out of line	5. Rape
6. Wearing improper clothing	6. Robbery
7. Not putting paper into the wastebasket	7. Assault

We are living in perilous times, and they have not

improved since 1980. The peril goes back directly to the ways in which people are violating God's ways. God designed authority for our protection. And while the removal of authority may get people what they want, it will also get them a host of things they don't want.

The other side of crumbling authority is that as parents have lost control, they also have become more violent. In a society where children have little respect for their parents, there is a marked increase in domestic violence and abuse. This complicates the issue, for on the surface, it seems to indicate the danger of authority. Thus, in an increasingly violent society, such disciplinary measures as spankings are being tossed out because they are thought to "increase the violent tendencies of children." When spankings are given in a fit of anger, no doubt they are counterproductive. Authority certainly can be abusive and improper.

What we need is a return to Biblical guidelines—parents exercising their authority in love, children honoring their parents.

Study Questions

1. How does Paul describe the last days? What specifically does he note that concerns us in this lesson?

2. What are some evidences that parents and teachers fear their children?

3. As you study the list of top problems in schools in 1940 and 1980, what conclusions can you draw? What may be other factors that contribute to this shift besides breakdown in parental authority? How, for example, may the influence of television be a factor? or the increased emphasis on pleasure

and material things? or shifts in ideologies in society (emphasis on pleasure, self-expression, self-love, or developing inner potential)? or the breakdown of marriages?

4. What abuses of authority have increased along with a general deterioration of authority? Why is this confusing?

5. What is the current view about spanking children? What verses in the Bible show us this is not true?

6. What factors can make spanking counterproductive?

APPLYING THE SCRIPTURE

1. How careful should we be in obeying civil laws? Is it wrong, for example, to travel several miles over the speed limit because policemen normally extend a few miles per hour of grace? What are the potential dangers of pushing the limits of laws?

2. What are the signs that authority is breaking down in our society?

3. How has the breakdown in authority in our society affected the church?

4. Why is it difficult to see the protective value of being under authority? What are some of the heartaches you have experienced or observed when people remove themselves from the protection of their authority figures?

5. Are there other examples in the Bible of those who resisted authority and experienced trouble as a direct result? What lessons can we learn from them?

6. What are the ties between rebellion and the occult?

7. To what extent have you been influenced by rock music? by your friends? Do you see rock music as wrong? Do you see "Christian rock" as presenting moral confusion? If your answer is no, you should study the New Testament Scriptures on music and talk with your parents or ministers.

8. To what extent have you demonstrated an independent spirit in regards to authority figures in your life? Have you personally seen the value of being under authority? Are there authority figures you need to be reconciled to? How have you justified yourself? What steps might you take at this point—does the story of the prodigal son give you any clues?

9. How do people sometimes try to create a conflict between human authority and God so they don't have to obey? Can a person, in other words, discount commands or advice of parents simply because they are not living right with the Lord and are not qualified to give advice?

10. How is the willingness to suffer an indication of whether we have a right spirit in obeying God rather than man?

11. What are some practical ways an adult Christian can honor unsaved parents?

12. What are the guidelines for making an appeal? What evidences are there that many Christians don't know how to appeal to authority?

1. John Blanchard, *Pop Goes the Gospel,* Evangelical Press, 1983, p. 55.

2. Ibid., p. 55.

Lesson 8

Faith and Feeling

INTRODUCTION

"When the Son of man cometh, shall he find faith on the earth?" (Luke 18:8). Jesus asked this question while teaching on the subject of not losing heart in prayer. We wonder what may have been on His heart with this question. Did He have in mind specific conditions of the endtimes that would make faith difficult? Was He recognizing that people would become so mindful of the physical and material world that their eyes would grow dim to the spiritual world? We wonder.

Certainly, in our time, true faith seems rare.

Although Christians know there is a spiritual realm, many seem to have a hard time distinguishing between spiritual fact and fancy. It is easy to rely on our feelings, to judge an event or a sermon or an activity by how we feel about it, to make important decisions largely on our inner feelings, or even to judge our spiritual condition basically by our feelings.

Our feelings are important. The inner workings of the Spirit do affect how we feel, but we easily confuse our feelings with the working of the Spirit, and especially so when faith is weak.

This lesson will explore the Biblical call to faith and see how faith helps us accurately weigh our feelings.

PERSONAL INVENTORY

1. Do you sometimes struggle with doubts and fears? If so, what specifically do you struggle with?

2. Do you know others who have struggled with doubts?

3. If someone were to come to you and be seriously questioning whether he was saved, what steps would you take to help that person?

4. Do you regularly exercise faith? In what way?
   By Believing in His promises that I
5. According to the Bible, there are different degrees *not* of faith. Do you feel comfortable with your faith *seen.* as it is? If not, what specifically do you think ought to be different?

6. In the Bible, what is to you the most outstanding example of faith? *Jesus - and Joseph*

SCRIPTURAL BACKGROUND

Now faith is the substance of things hoped for, the evidence of things not seen. Without faith it is impossible to please him: for he that cometh to God must believe that he is, and that he is a rewarder of them that diligently seek him. Hebrews 11:1, 6.

So then faith cometh by hearing, and hearing by the word of God. Romans 10:17.

The fruit of the Spirit is . . . faith. Galatians 5:22.

Then said I, Ah, Lord God! behold, I cannot speak: for I am a child. But the LORD *said unto me, Say not, I am a child: for thou shalt go to all that I shall send thee, and whatsoever I command thee thou shalt speak. Be not afraid of their faces: for I am with thee to deliver thee, saith the* LORD. Jeremiah 1:6-8.

And when the servant of the man of God was risen early, and gone forth, behold, an host compassed the city both with horses and chariots. And his servant said unto him, Alas, my master! how shall we do? And he answered, Fear not: for they that be with us are more than they that be with them. And Elisha prayed, and said, LORD, *I pray thee, open his eyes, that he may see. And the* LORD *opened the eyes of the young man; and he saw: and, behold, the mountain was full of horses and chariots of fire round about Elisha.* 2 Kings 6:15-17.

For God hath not given us the spirit of fear; but of power, and of love, and of a sound mind. 2 Timothy 1:7.

And straightway the father of the child cried out, and said with tears, Lord, I believe; help thou mine unbelief. Mark 9:24.

My little children, let us not love in word, neither in tongue; but in deed and in truth. And hereby we know that we are of the truth, and shall assure our hearts before him. For if our heart condemn us, God is greater than our heart, and knoweth all things. Beloved, if our heart condemn us not, then have we confidence toward God. 1 John 3:18-21.

And now, behold, I go bound in the spirit unto

Jerusalem, not knowing the things that shall befall me there: Save that the Holy Ghost witnesseth in every city, saying that bonds and afflictions abide me. . . . And now, behold, I know that ye all, among whom I have gone preaching the kingdom of God, shall see my face no more. Acts 20:22, 23, 25.

Beloved, believe not every spirit, but try the spirits whether they are of God: because many false prophets are gone out into the world. 1 John 4:1.

UNDERSTANDING THE SCRIPTURES

> *Now faith is the substance of things hoped for, the evidence of things not seen. Without faith it is impossible to please him: for he that cometh to God must believe that he is, and that he is a rewarder of them that diligently seek him.* Hebrews 11:1, 6.

OBSERVATION #1: *Faith is a certainty about unseen spiritual realities.*

We live in a physical, material world. We have senses that operate and respond largely on the physical, material level—sight, hearing, touch, smell, and taste. Scientists are finding out that the material world is extremely complex. They continue to explore and discover new territory. Unfortunately, the more we focus on the material world, the more difficult it seems for many people to realize there are unseen realities. An angel cannot be studied under a microscope. No scientist can discover the molecular structure of prayer. He has no beaker that can measure the power of God.

Heavenly realities are not subject to our sight or our touch. But they are nonetheless real, and we must accept them.

How?

By faith. Faith is the certainty that there are spiritual realities as described by the Bible, and it is the willingness on the part of man to act upon those realities. In the natural world, we know that walking down a house roof will bring us to the edge, and stepping beyond the edge will result in a fall to the ground. We trust our senses and our understanding of the natural laws and thus avoid such tumbles. In the spiritual world, we are told that the result of sin is death. We cannot see sin as a spiritual object. We cannot see the fall into sin or feel the death at the bottom of the fall. We cannot see how God and the angels and the devil and his hosts all have their part in that law of sin. So by nature we tend to ignore the law. Faith says, "Pay attention! When you sin, you are setting in motion a spiritual law that is just as real as the law of gravity! Since you are fallen, you need to be rescued as much as any worker who has ever fallen from a roof!" Faith operates by the laws and realities of the unseen spiritual realm.

OBSERVATION #2: It is impossible to come to God or to please Him without faith.

God is the ultimate spiritual reality. He is the Source of all things material and spiritual. When we encounter Him, we encounter the Author, the Source, the One "upholding all things by the word of his power" (Hebrews 1:3). Until we encounter God, we will be confused about the rest of reality.

Encountering God, however, is not like bumping into an acquaintance downtown. God is Spirit. There is no touching Him, seeing Him, or hearing Him. There is only believing Him. He will evidence Himself to us in a multitude of ways once we believe, but he who comes must believe. Once the eyes of faith are opened, all things take on a different perspective. Seeing ourselves in the light of God is altogether different from seeing ourselves in the mirror. Seeing the world in the light of God is altogether different from driving downtown on a Saturday night. How we need the light of God! But without faith, we remain spiritually blind, spiritually ignorant, spiritually dead.

Study Questions

1. How is faith defined in Hebrews 11:1? Read this verse in other translations. What insights do you receive?

2. What other Scriptures can you find that define faith or its importance?

3. Why does the exploration of the physical world seem to be so often accompanied by a departure from faith? *Because we often believe only what we see*

4. List some spiritual realities we cannot see.

5. State some spiritual laws.

6. Why is faith indispensable in coming to God?

7. According to Hebrews 11:6, what two things are we to believe by faith when we come to God? *Believe that He is and that He rewards those who seek Him.*

8. How does faith in God change all of our perspective? *It gives us peace + assurance.*

9. What is the effect of not believing in God? *loss of peace + fullfillment*

144

> *So then faith cometh by hearing, and hearing by the word of God.* Romans 10:17.
>
> *The fruit of the Spirit is . . . faith.* Galatians 5:22.

OBSERVATION #3: Faith is nurtured by the Word and by the indwelling Spirit.

Since faith is so important, how do we get it? Faith is not natural to us in our fallen state. We must hear the Word of God. This is what makes preaching so imperative—not merely the formal preaching behind a pulpit, but the testimony of believers, the Gospel passed by word of mouth on the job and in the marketplace. Faith is stirred in the hearts of people as they hear what God has said and done. How we need proclaimers of the Word today!

The same law operates in the heart after faith has come. Faith may be weak at the beginning. It may be immature. It may be only a seed. Faith needs the continuing input of the Word of God to grow. As believers hear the Word, they become stronger believers. Faith comes by hearing the Word.

Faith is also described as the fruit of the Spirit in the life of the believer. The Holy Spirit is unseen. His residence in us is spiritual, not tangible. As we learn to walk in step with Him, He opens our eyes of faith more and more to the realm we cannot see with our natural eyes. And we learn to "walk by faith, not by sight" (2 Corinthians 5:7). Spiritual insight is not the product of mere study, and it is not a matter of superior intellect; it comes to those whose hearts are tuned to God. The

145

man who has an IQ of 95 who walks with God will have greater spiritual sense, will exercise more faith, and will be more pleasing to God than a godless genius. Faith comes through the indwelling Spirit.

Study Questions

1. List the sequence presented in Romans 10:17. This verse is parallel to a sequence given in verses 14 and 15. List the sequence there. (It is given in reverse order.) What is meant by preaching in this passage?

2. In your own words state the place of the Word of God in relation to faith.

3. How does faith grow? Staying in the Word - Walking with & believing God.

4. Can you give examples of weak faith from the Bible? Sarah - by giving Hagar to Abram.

5. How does the Holy Spirit produce faith in us? Dwells in us - draws us to God -

6. Why is it important to view faith as the product of the Holy Spirit? What are some of the things people might mistake for faith in a person's life? Strong personality traits.

7. What examples in the Bible are there of ordinary people with a strong faith? What is admirable about their lives? Joseph - Ruth

Now that we have looked at faith, let's consider our feelings. What do we mean by feelings? We do not mean the sense of touch. Rather, we mean our emotions, the moods within us that give color to what we do and say and think. Feelings are powerful forces in our lives. We like positive feelings such as peace, happiness, confidence, and security; and we don't like negative feelings like discouragement, fear, and doubt. These emotions are deeper than our physical senses, and because they are deeper, we are prone to mistake them for what is deeper still—the working of the Spirit of God in us.

For many Christians, it is far easier to live by our feelings than by faith. In the material that follows, we will examine five common areas where Christians struggle with their feelings. We will allow the Word of God to illuminate the issues and show us how to handle these feelings.

DISCOURAGEMENT

> *Then said I, Ah, Lord God! behold, I cannot speak: for I am a child. But the LORD said unto me, Say not, I am a child: for thou shalt go to all that I shall send thee, and whatsoever I command thee thou shalt speak. Be not afraid of their faces: for I am with thee to deliver thee, saith the LORD.*
> Jeremiah 1:6-8.

Have you ever felt discouraged? Most people do at some time or another.

In the text above, Jeremiah felt like a little child. He had a hard assignment—to be a prophet to a rebellious people—and he felt inadequate and discouraged before he even started. Ten of the twelve spies had a similar perspective when they checked out the land of Canaan. Comparing the walled cities and the giants of Anak with their resources—an

Discouragement *is the result of comparing a difficult task with inadequate resources.*

untrained army of normal-sized men—they felt inadequate . . . and discouraged.

What Jeremiah and the ten spies were not taking into account was the presence of the Lord. God wasn't calling Jeremiah to be a prophet by himself. God promised to be with him. God wasn't sending the Israelites into Canaan by themselves. He intended to go before them. But we can't *see* God. That is where faith comes in. As Jeremiah believed in God, he no longer viewed his task as hopeless. The two spies who believed in God were confident they could go into the land of Canaan. As Christians, we regularly face tasks that are too large for us. Only the exercise of faith will keep us from discouragement.

When we feel discouraged, we must not operate by our feelings. We must focus our spiritual vision on the Lord and walk forward by faith. There was a time when David's men were muttering about stoning him and David felt alone and

> *Courage is the result of believing that God is with me in the tasks He has given me to do.*

discouraged, but the Bible says he "encouraged himself in the LORD his God" (1 Samuel 30:6). By focusing on the Lord, David was living by faith, not by his feelings. The Lord honored David's faith and helped him through this difficult time. "And this is the victory that overcometh the world, even our faith" (1 John 5:4).

hallelujah!

Study Questions

1. How did Jeremiah feel? What task did he have? How did the Lord encourage him? *With assurance that he was with Him*

2. What is discouragement?

3. What other examples are there in the Bible of people who were discouraged? For each example, tell what mental comparisons the people were making that made them discouraged. *Moses, John the Baptist*

4. Why is faith necessary in overcoming discouragement? What are people not usually seeing when they are discouraged? *That God is with us— His Grace is sufficient.*

5. How did David overcome discouragement? What do you think he did specifically? (What clues do his Psalms give us?) *He cried out to God.*

6. What is courage? *Believing God, believing we are who he says we are, believing He is who He says he is. Believing He will do what He says He will.*

7. What are some Biblical examples of courage? *Joshua, Abraham, Paul*

FEAR

> *And when the servant of the man of God was risen early, and gone forth, behold, an host compassed the city both with horses and chariots. And his servant said unto him, Alas, my master! how shall we do? And he answered, Fear not: for they that be with us are more than they that be with them. And Elisha prayed, and said, LORD, I pray thee, open his eyes, that he may see. And the LORD opened the eyes of the young man; and he saw: and, behold, the mountain was full of horses and chariots of fire round about Elisha.* 2 Kings 6:15-17.
>
> *For God hath not given us the spirit of fear; but of power, and of love, and of a sound mind.* 2 Timothy 1:7.

Fear is another emotion we sometimes struggle with. Like discouragement, it keeps us from doing what needs to be done.

When Elisha's servant saw the Syrian army around the city, he was terrified. "Alas, my master! how shall we do?" was his cry. The servant could see the danger, but he could not see the protection of the Lord, and he was naturally afraid. In the New Testament, Timothy was

> **Fear** *is the emotional result of facing danger or great difficulty without a sense of protection.*

a young bishop who faced many difficulties as a church leader. By nature, Timothy seemed to shrink from these problems. Difficulties may expose us—may show us up as weak or inadequate. Through difficulties, people may come to not like us. We don't know all that may have been in Timothy's mind, but Paul often encourages him not to fear. "God hath not given us the spirit of fear!" When we are afraid, we can know this is not from God—our feelings are in charge, and by faith we must rise above them.

Elisha did not pray that God would remove the danger of the Syrian army. He only prayed that God would open the eyes of the servant. When the servant saw the mountain filled with the fiery hosts of the Lord, he realized he was fully protected in this time of danger. Paul did not tell Timothy that God would help him avoid difficulties. Rather, he assured Timothy of the indwelling Spirit of power that God has given us. The spiritual hosts of the Lord are unseen. The indwelling Spirit is unseen. We can be assured of these spiritual realities only by faith.

When by faith we understand the Lord's protection, fear can be turned to confidence. We view the danger no longer from the standpoint of feeling unprotected and vulnerable but from the vantage point of knowing we are surrounded and shielded by the Almighty.

When our confidence is the confidence of faith, we no longer need to be controlled by the feeling of fear. We can face danger and difficulty by faith in God's perfect protection. "If God be for us, who can be against us? . . . Who shall separate us from the love of Christ?

> **Confidence** is the realization that those who follow God's will are protected by God's hand.

shall tribulation, or distress, or persecution, or famine, or nakedness, or peril, or sword? . . . Nay, in all these things we are more than conquerors through him that loved us. For I am persuaded, that neither death, nor life, nor angels, nor principalities, nor powers, nor things present, nor things to come, nor height, nor depth, nor any other creature, shall be able to separate us from the love of God, which is in Christ Jesus" (Romans 8:31-39).

Study Questions

1. What danger did Elisha's servant see? Was it a real danger? *Yes*

2. What protection did Elisha's servant not see? Was it a real protection? *yes*

3. What was Elisha's prayer for his servant? *That His eyes would be opened to spiritual realities*

4. How did the situation turn out?

5. What difficulty did Timothy face as a church leader? What fears might he have had? List other verses from Paul's letters to Timothy that are encouraging.

151

6. What is fear?

7. What may be God's purposes for not always removing us from danger? *to test &* *strengthen our faith.*

8. How do we suffer? List some of the things Paul suffered. Where is God's protection when Christians suffer? What light does Matthew 10:28-31 give on this question? *God will always provide what we need, not want.*

9. List the assurances given in Romans 8:31-39. *Nothing shall seperate us from God's Love*

10. What is confidence? How is confidence as defined here different from cockiness? *We are resting in God's provision.*

DOUBT

> *And straightway the father of the child cried out, and said with tears, Lord, I believe; help thou mine unbelief.* Mark 9:24.

As a feeling, doubt stands opposed to the action of faith. To understand doubt, we need to clearly understand faith. In Hebrews 11, we read about many people of faith. How do we know they were people of faith? By their *actions*. Faith must be understood not only by what it is, but also by what it does. Recall the verbs in Hebrews 11? By faith Abel offered. By faith Noah *moved with fear*. By faith Abraham *went out*. By faith Abraham *offered up* Isaac. By faith Moses *refused . . . choosing* rather to *suffer . . . esteeming* the reproach of Christ . . . *forsook* Egypt . . . *endured*. We are not saying that what we think and feel has nothing to do with faith, but we are saying that what we *do* has more to do with faith than what we *feel*.

Thus, the feeling of doubt sometimes accompanies the action of faith. Doubt makes the difference between a strong faith and a weak faith. The more doubts we have, the weaker will be our faith. Doubts undermine faith. The less doubts we have, the stronger our faith. We need not assume that the people in Hebrews 11 had no doubts, but we can know that they acted in spite of them. What they did was more important than how they felt.

We see the struggle in the father of the possessed child. He expressed his faith and confessed his unbelief in the same exclamation. "I believe, but help!" Unfortunately, the disciples, who had seen Jesus perform many miracles and who had performed miracles themselves, did not have a strong enough faith for this situation. We see at other times that though they believed Jesus could heal the sick, they were astonished that He could still the storm. Though He raised the dead, they could not comprehend that He Himself would rise from the dead.

> **Doubt** is the human limitation I place on divine power or authority.

We are much like the father of the boy and like the disciples. We believe in a God we can understand. We are able to believe Him when He acts according to our expectations. But we have trouble actually believing in "him that is able to do exceeding abundantly above all that we ask or think" (Ephesians 3:20).

Doubt undermines faith in many ways. Zacharias doubted when the angel told him his wife would have a son. Peter doubted when the Lord told him in a vision to "kill and eat" unclean animals, that is, to accept the Gentiles. Noah could have doubted the wisdom of building a boat on the dry land. Abraham could have doubted the reasonableness of starting on a trip without knowing his destination, or of offering up a son he had received supernaturally. Faith calls us to rise above such doubts. When the Lord has a work to do, we must not place our limitations on how He ought to do it, or when, or to what extent we will be a part of it.

The doubt we have been discussing so far has to do with the work and will of God. Faith calls us to rise above the feelings of doubt we have about God's ability and authority. There is another kind of doubt, however, that the Bible tells us to treat differently. It is the doubt of conscience. In Romans 14, Paul says that some Jewish believers doubted their freedom to live above the Law, especially regarding the eating of certain food. And Paul told them not to disregard those doubts. He says, "The man who has doubts is condemned if he eats, because his eating is not from faith; and everything that does not come from faith is sin" (Romans 14:23, NIV).

> **Trust** is the inner conviction that God is fully able to do whatever is His will to do.

> **Trust** is the willingness to leave with God the full responsibility for His work.

Our conscience is a gift from God. It can be trained both rightly and wrongly, and fortunately, it can be retrained. But it should not be violated. When we come to the Lord, our conscience becomes an important inner guide in the hands of the

> **Trust** is the willingness to do whatever God asks of me in spite of doubts.

Holy Spirit. It becomes very sensitive to the Word and will of God. The life of faith is a life lived in harmony with this Spirit-controlled, Bible-trained conscience. So the doubt of conscience is different from the doubt of unbelief. When the Lord tells us to do something, we are to ignore our doubt feelings and act in faith. When our conscience warns us not to do something, however, we are to pay attention to those doubts, lest we violate our faith.

Study Questions

1. What is doubt? How does doubt affect faith?
   Not Trusting · It weakens our faith.
2. How is faith known? *By our actions*
3. How does Hebrews 11:33-35 illuminate our understanding of faith? *It requires action*
4. What is the difference between a weak faith and a strong faith? *Doubt*
5. What doubts might Noah have had? Abraham? Moses? *In Noahs time it had never yet rained.*
6. What examples do we have where the disciples of Jesus doubted? What examples do we have where they exercised faith? *feeding the 5000*
7. In what way do we see doubt mixed with faith in the father of the possessed boy? Why was his prayer a proper prayer? *It was honest*
8. List three evidences of trust. Give an example of each from the Bible. *Abraham moving - Joseph. requiring his bones to moved.*
9. How does the exercise of faith help us overcome doubt?
10. What kind of doubt does Paul discuss in Romans 14? *doubt of conscience*

Joshua - marching 7 times @ Jerico

155

11. How should we live in relation to our conscience?

12. How are we to respond to doubt feelings of unbelief regarding the Lord's power or authority?

    trust and have faith in God

13. How are we to respond to doubt feelings of conscience regarding right and wrong?

    follow the scripture & listen to the Spirit through our conscience

GUILT

> *My little children, let us not love in word, neither in tongue; but in deed and in truth. And hereby we know that we are of the truth, and shall assure our hearts before him. For if our heart condemn us, God is greater than our heart, and knoweth all things. Beloved, if our heart condemn us not, then have we confidence toward God. 1 John 3:18-21.*

Some Christians struggle with guilt feelings. Although they have repented from their sins, they continue to feel condemned. We cannot see our sin, and we cannot see our forgiveness. Therefore, the removal of our sin is something we must accept by faith, not by feeling.

Before we go on, however, we must clarify the difference between the condition of guilt and the feeling of guilt. When we sin, we ARE guilty. This is the condition of guilt, and it does not depend on our feelings. Many people sin and do not feel guilty. According to the Bible, all have sinned, and therefore all experience the condition of guilt. The feeling of guilt often accompanies the condition of guilt. It is what makes the sinner miserable, especially when he hears the truth. The feeling of guilt is often what drives the sinner finally to his knees. However, just as people can be guilty without feeling guilty, so sometimes people can feel guilty without actually being guilty. It is these guilt feelings we are dealing with here.

> **Guilt feelings** *persist when we focus only on how unworthy we are to be forgiven.*

Satan is a master of misrepresentation. He sometimes uses truth to lead us into error. It is true we are unworthy of God's forgiveness. That is one of the reasons He chose to provide for our forgiveness—we never could have. But it is error to conclude that because we are unworthy, we are not forgiven. Apparently many people struggled with their feelings in John's day, for he wrote numerous tests by which people can be assured that they are God's children, or be shown that they are not. The test of love is one he describes in this passage. By the exercise of love, we "shall assure our hearts before him." But sometimes our hearts still condemn us, even though we have confessed our sins, though we obey God, though we have received the anointing of the Holy Spirit, and though we walk in love toward others. We get to looking at our past sins, or we get to thinking about our present struggles, our weaknesses, and our failures; and suddenly, we see what wretched people we are outside of Christ. Feelings of guilt come over us.

God calls us to focus instead on thankfulness. Feelings of unworthiness should be a call to praise, not a route to despondency. Our unworthiness is exactly what makes God's forgiveness so full of grace and glory.

The Apostle Paul "was before a blasphemer, and a persecutor, and injurious," but "the grace of our Lord was exceeding abundant with faith and love which is in Christ Jesus." Paul says his wicked past, so gloriously forgiven through the mercy of Jesus, was to be a demonstration to all what wretched people God can save. (See 1 Timothy 1:13-16.)

Rising above our guilt feelings is an exercise of faith. It is a refocusing from ourselves to the Lord, from our unworthiness to His mercy.

Three truths are important in settling the matter of our forgiveness:

1. Forgiveness is based on *God's Word.* We are forgiven because God says so in His Word (Psalm 130:3, 4; Colossians 2:13; 1 John 2:12, etc.). I CAN BELIEVE WHAT GOD HAS SAID.

2. Forgiveness is based on *Jesus' shed blood.* If God received the blood of animals under the Old Testament, will He not much more receive the blood of His own Son as full atonement for sin? (See Hebrews 9:13, 14.) God is not playing games. When He provided for our forgiveness, He made the provision certain. I CAN TRUST IN JESUS' SACRIFICE FOR ME.

3. The ability to *receive* forgiveness depends much upon the willingness to *extend* forgiveness. Sometimes we struggle with extending forgiveness because we are not willing to forgive. Jesus taught us that if we want to receive forgiveness, we must extend it (Matthew 6:14, 15; and 18:21-35). AS I PRACTICE EXTENDING FORGIVENESS TO OTHERS, I BECOME FREE TO RECEIVE FORGIVENESS MYSELF.

The result of exercising faith and rising above guilt feelings is peace. As we focus on the Lord in gratitude, as we extend forgiveness to others, the peace of God fills our hearts.

> *Peace is the result of gratefully resting the forgiveness of my sins entirely on the merits of Christ.*

Study Questions

1. What are realities we cannot see in the process of receiving forgiveness?

2. What is the difference between the condition of guilt and guilt feelings? How can we be deceived about both?

3. What is the value of guilt feelings?

4. What causes guilt feelings to persist when we have been forgiven? How is this based on truth? How is it wrong?

5. What are some of the tests John gives to assure believers?

6. What does John say is greater than what our hearts say?

7. Is it wrong to feel unworthy of God's forgiveness? What would be the effect of feeling worthy? What should our unworthiness cause in us?

8. How is Paul's conversion a testimony of God's mercy? What are some of the wicked things he did before conversion?

9. List three truths that are the basis for rising in faith above guilt feelings. What is the result of exercising faith for forgiveness?

10. Define peace in contrast to guilt feelings. Find some Scriptures that support this understanding of peace.

IMPRESSIONS

> *And now, behold, I go bound in the spirit unto Jerusalem, not knowing the things that shall befall me there: Save that the Holy Ghost witnesseth in every city, saying that bonds and afflictions abide me. . . . And now, behold, I know that ye all, among whom I have gone preaching the kingdom of God, shall see my face no more.* Acts 20:22, 23, 25.
>
> *Beloved, believe not every spirit, but try the spirits whether they are of God: because many false prophets are gone out into the world.* 1 John 4:1.

In the above Scripture from Acts, we find Paul apparently hearing the inner voice of the Spirit. And we could note many similar examples throughout the Book of Acts. Does the Lord still speak through that inner voice? And how can we tell whether it is the Lord speaking or simply a feeling or thought that popped into our minds at a certain time? These questions are especially troubling to young Christians.

Not having discernment can lead to very unfortunate situations. A young man may receive a clear inner impression that he is to marry a young girl only to find that she has a very decided impression otherwise. A person may experience a strong urging to shout something aloud in a public meeting, or do something else that seems utterly bizarre. Hearing how God did something very strange in someone else's life may make a sincere Christian susceptible to these inner urgings, especially if he has just made a commitment to be totally devoted to the Lord and not to fear man.

Just how do we distinguish these inner feelings and impressions from the leading of the Spirit? Finding answers here is not always as black and white as we might wish. There is strong evidence, for example, that even Paul, in the above example, mixed his own impressions with the voice of the Spirit.

Principles of Holy Spirit Direction

1. The Holy Spirit honors certain channels in giving His direction.

God's Word stands as a continuing message from the Spirit. If we want to have the leading of the Spirit in our lives, we must be in the Word regularly. God speaks to those who are in tune with Him.

It is true that before the New Testament was written, or where the Bible is scarce, or people cannot read, God may give special revelations to His people. But those who have the Word are wise to seek the mind of the Spirit through that Word. Other spiritual channels are prayer, counsel from authority figures, and the fellowship of the saints. As we focus on hearing what God says in His Word, on what He tells us on our knees, on what He tells us through the counsel of our leaders, and on what He tells us through the brotherhood, we have a basis for evaluating the inner voices we hear— whether they really are of the Spirit or whether they are merely our own imagination.

2. *Discerning the voice of the Spirit requires spiritual maturity.*

Often young Christians have trouble with understanding inner impressions. Usually, these are sincere Christians, willing to do God's will, but confused about His voice. Again, this is good reason to focus on the more certain channels of God's voice—His Word, counsel from authority, and counsel from the brotherhood. This doesn't mean God cannot speak to spiritual babies, but it takes time to learn the language of the Spirit.

As mentioned earlier, Paul may have misinterpreted what the Spirit told him. Notice, the Holy Spirit told him that "bonds and afflictions" were waiting for him. Paul then told the Ephesian elders that he knew he would see their faces no more. Did the Holy Spirit tell him that, or did he conclude that from what the Holy Spirit did tell him? There is strong evidence in piecing together Paul's last letters that he did again travel through Asia, likely after being released from Rome. What the Spirit had said was true, but Paul may have misunderstood the implications.

In any case, the Apostle John's warning to "try the spirits" indicates that misunderstanding and even deception are possible. Young Christians should be especially careful about basing their ideas or decisions on inner impressions alone.

3. *The Holy Spirit honors Christ.*

The leading of the Spirit, as we observe it in the Book of Acts, was always associated with carrying forth the Gospel. Those who were sent out were sent out by the direction of the Spirit (Acts 13). As they went, they relied heavily on the Spirit's guidance. We can be sure they spent much time in prayer, even in fasting, in seeking that guidance. Wherever Christ is being lifted up, the guidance and anointing of the Spirit are necessary. Many people today would like the Spirit's direction for business decisions, for purchasing and selling, for investments, etc. Unless those decisions are for the advancement of Christ and His kingdom, we have good reason to doubt whether the direction of the Holy Spirit will be in it. The Holy Spirit is given to honor Christ, not so that we may use Him as a tool to make us rich or happy or comfortable.

When we focus on inner impressions, we easily move away from guidance by faith to guidance by feeling. We may neglect the Word. We may ignore the counsel of authority God has placed over us. We may ignore spiritual fellowship and the shaping work of brotherhood. Guidance by feeling leaves us open to spiritual danger.

Dangers of Following Our Feelings

1. Seeking after signs.

To some people it seems exciting to be able to relate spectacular stories of special signs and voices and visions. Unfortunately, at the bottom of this is human pride, rather than the glory of God.

2. Avoiding the responsibility of making decisions.

Christians need to make decisions, sometimes very difficult decisions. Sometimes we seek an inner word from the Lord or a sign to determine what we ought to do. If we are not careful, we may simply be attempting to avoid the responsibility of making a decision ourselves, trying to hear an inner voice rather than wisely weighing what we are facing.

3. Using "The Lord told me _____" as a means of bolstering our own thoughts or actions.

This can be subtle. Who wants to argue with us if we

163

say the Lord told us to do a certain thing? Thus, we can consciously or subconsciously hide our actions from evaluation.

4. *Opening oneself indiscriminately to the spiritual realm.*

Probably the biggest danger of a focus on inner impressions is that we open ourselves to voices that are not from the Lord. There are many spirits besides the Holy Spirit who are eager to speak to us. Paul warned, "Now the Spirit speaketh expressly, that in the latter times some shall depart from the faith, giving heed to seducing spirits, and doctrines of devils" (1 Timothy 4:1). John tells us to "try the spirits whether they be of God" (1 John 4:1).

The direction of the Holy Spirit in the lives of those who are honoring Christ is precious beyond measure. We are thrilled reading the Book of Acts to see how He guided the work of the church. And it is proper to seek the inner guidance of the same Spirit today. But we must beware of abuses and counterfeits.

Study Questions

1. What was the Holy Spirit telling Paul in Acts 20:23? What did Paul conclude in verse 25?

2. List at least five other examples of the Holy Spirit guiding people in the Book of Acts.

3. What are some unfortunate things that can happen when a person mistakes his own ideas for the voice of the Holy Spirit?

4. List the ways the Holy Spirit provides guidance other than through an inner voice. Why is it important to test our inner urgings by these other channels of His direction?

5. How does the natural learning of language illustrate the spiritual?

6. What is the significance of knowing that the Holy Spirit's directions will honor Christ? What verses in John 16 state this principle?

7. How do people try to use the Spirit's direction for selfish interests?

8. What is the effect of focusing on inner impressions as a primary means of discerning the leading of the Spirit? List four dangers of such a focus.

9. Describe the blessings of being led by the Spirit. Why is it so necessary to beware of counterfeit inner guidance?

APPLYING THE SCRIPTURE

1. How do you feel about your personal faith? Would you describe your faith as weak or strong? If weak, what sort of doubts do you have?

2. Considering the principle that faith comes by the Word, describe the place of the Word of God in your life in relation to your faith. Are there ways you could be getting more exposure to the Word to increase your faith?

3. Considering that faith is a product of the Holy Spirit, how might you increase your faith? What place does the Holy Spirit have in your life? Do you walk in step with Him?

4. What are some situations in your life where you have been discouraged? What were you comparing in your mind?

5. What are some practical ways to encourage oneself in the Lord (as David did)?

6. What kinds of fears have you (or people close to you) had? To what extent have you struggled with the following fears? Fear of man? Fear of failure? Fear of exposure? Fear of rejection? Fear of fear?

7. What are some situations where fear is legitimate? Is the Lord's protection automatic, in other words, or is it limited to those who are in His will? How did Satan attempt to get Jesus to trust a promise of God presumptuously? (See Matthew 4:6.)

8. In what way have you put limitations on God's power and authority? How might the Lord be calling you to greater trust?

9. What is the difference between faith and presumption? How are people presumptuous today?

10. What are ways in which individual consciences vary? Why is it important to honor our conscience? To what extent should we honor another person's conscience? Is there a balance, in other words, between honoring another person's conscience and being controlled by others?

11. Have you struggled with guilt feelings? Why is it important to be certain of thorough repentance before trying to rise above guilt feelings? Why is it dangerous to seek God's forgiveness repeatedly for sins of the past?

12. Have you followed inner urgings that you felt were the leading of the Spirit? What blessings have you received? Have you done this and later questioned whether it actually was His leading?

13. Why are young Christians especially susceptible to a wrong emphasis on inner urgings? How do older Christians sometimes contribute to misunderstanding?

14. Having studied this lesson, how would you describe the place of faith in the believer? How would you describe the place of feelings? What do you feel are some necessary steps in your own life for increasing faith?

Bitterness and Forgiveness

INTRODUCTION

We live in a hurting world. People are hurt in marriage, people are hurt in childhood, people are hurt in the work world, people are hurt in school, and people are hurt in the church. Were we able to see the souls of people, we would no doubt see scars on everyone. It is impossible to live a hurt-free life.

Not everyone responds to hurts in the same way. Some seem to pass hurts off easily. Some people have hurts that have festered for years. They have sores all over and "ouch" at the slightest touch. Others have hidden their hurts away. On the surface they appear healed, even callous. But underneath, they have pain so buried they hardly feel it themselves. Yet it affects them. In their attitudes and in their responses, they favor that sore spot.

In this lesson, we want to examine not only hurts, but ways of finding healing. The Bible is not silent on this issue, and we do well to pay close attention, because the consequence of not dealing rightly with hurts is bitterness. And bitterness is a cancer that destroys the whole person.

PERSONAL INVENTORY

1. Have you ever been deeply angry with particular people or about particular situations in your life? What have you done about it?

2. Do you find yourself mentally reviewing painful things that have happened in the past?

3. Do you find yourself arguing with particular people in your mind; that is, going over old arguments you have had, and inventing new arguments? Who usually wins?

4. Have you ever had to struggle to forgive someone? Were you able to forgive, or do you continue to struggle?

5. What does it mean to you to forgive?

6. What helpful pointers have you learned to enable you to forgive?

SCRIPTURAL BACKGROUND

Be ye angry, and sin not: let not the sun go down upon your wrath: Neither give place to the devil. . . . And grieve not the holy Spirit of God, whereby ye are sealed unto the day of redemption. Let all bitterness, and wrath, and anger, and clamour, and evil speaking, be put away from you, with all malice: And be ye kind one to another, tenderhearted, forgiving one another, even as God for Christ's sake hath forgiven you. Ephesians 4:26, 27, 30-32.

Follow peace with all men, and holiness, without which no man shall see the Lord: Looking diligently lest any man fail of the grace of God; lest any root of bitterness springing up trouble you, and thereby many be defiled. Hebrews 12:14, 15.

Then said he unto the disciples, It is impossible but that offences will come: but woe unto him, through whom they come! It were better for him that a millstone were hanged about his neck, and he cast into the sea, than that he should offend one of these little ones. Take heed to yourselves: If thy brother trespass against thee, rebuke him; and if he repent, forgive him. And if he trespass against thee seven times in a day, and seven times in a day turn again to thee, saying, I repent; thou shalt forgive him. And the apostles said unto the Lord, Increase our faith. Luke 17:1-5.

Then came Peter to him, and said, Lord, how oft shall my brother sin against me, and I forgive him? till seven times? Jesus saith unto him, I say not unto thee, Until seven times: but, Until seventy times seven. Matthew 18:21, 22.

For if ye forgive men their trespasses, your heavenly Father will also forgive you: But if ye forgive not men their trespasses, neither will your Father forgive your trespasses. Matthew 6:14, 15.

UNDERSTANDING THE SCRIPTURES

> *Be ye angry, and sin not: let not the sun go down upon your wrath: Neither give place to the devil. . . . And grieve not the holy Spirit of God, whereby ye are sealed unto the day of redemption. Let all bitterness, and wrath, and anger, and clamour, and evil speaking, be put away from you, with all malice: And be ye kind one to another, tenderhearted, forgiving one another, even as God for Christ's sake hath forgiven you.* Ephesians 4:26-32.

OBSERVATION #1: Anger is a dangerous emotion.

The exact meaning of the first part of verse 26 is debated. The NIV avoids the command form in the Greek (Be angry) and renders the verse: "In your anger, do not sin." Anger, like any other emotion, rises as an emotional response to situations, and therefore, like other emotions, anger is to a certain extent involuntary. We don't decide to be sad or happy or sympathetic or angry. These are emotions that involuntarily respond to what we are experiencing. But recognizing that emotions are involuntary does not mean we have no control over them. We do. We may be angry enough to bite railroad spikes in two when suddenly the phone rings. At once, we answer as though we had just read Psalm 23. We not only *can* control these emotions, but we are *responsible* to control them, and particularly the way we express them.

Thus, we have the command, "Sin not." What we do with our anger is our responsibility. We think wrongly when we think others made us sin. Others may do wrong. We may become angry. But if we sin, we bear the responsibility. In your anger, *do not sin!*

Since the command not to sin comes right on the heels of the statement on anger, we can assume that where anger rises, sin is never far away. Therefore we must be extra careful with this emotion. It is dangerously close to sin. We could well wonder how much sin has been done in the heat of anger. We have but to look in our own lives to see how quickly the emotion of anger moves to the action of sin.

Anger that burns and burns in the heart over a period of time is destructive. It destroys the mind, the disposition, the spirit, and even the body.

OBSERVATION #2: The Christian is obligated to control his anger.

We have already alluded to this, but we look at it further because much misunderstanding surrounds this concept. Modern psychologists, seeing the destructive effects of anger, have suggested nonviolent expressions of anger. "Don't hold anger inside," they counsel. "And don't beat up your brother or throw books through the living room window. Rather, go outside and run a mile, or go upstairs and beat a pillow. Once you've vented your anger, you can deal constructively with your problem."

The difficulty with this "solution" is that venting anger even in nonviolent ways can intensify anger patterns. The Bible says, "He that is slow to anger is better than the mighty; and he that ruleth his spirit than he that taketh a city" (Proverbs 16:32). It is wise to control anger. It is unwise to vent it or to let it take charge of our actions. In the verses from Ephesians, we are told

173

to put away anger. Obviously, this means we have responsibility. Before we look at how to control anger, we need to study this emotion more closely.

OBSERVATION #3: *Anger that is retained for long periods of time is especially destructive.*

"Let not the sun go down upon your wrath: Neither give place to the devil." We can assume that carrying over anger from one day to the next gives the devil a foothold in our lives. Why? Anger that is retained turns into bitterness, and bitterness has a host of attendant sins that please the devil immensely—malice, grudges, ill will, suspicion, slander, gossip, murmuring, blame shifting, self-pity. There is probably no inner attitude more destructive than that of bitterness. It poisons the heart and robs it of joy. It shrivels the mind to thinking in the same dreary circles day after day. "A wounded spirit who can bear?" (Proverbs 18:14). If anger carried over from one day to another is dangerous, how much more that which is carried over from year to year, and *how much more* that which is passed on from one generation to the next? Let not the sun go down upon your wrath!

The devil does great damage in people who are bitter for years. He does even more damage when fathers and mothers pass on their anger to their children. Only the grace of God can break these chains of sin.

Study Questions

1. List the commands regarding anger in these verses.

2. Why is the exact meaning of "Be ye angry" debated? How does the NIV translate this expression? How do other translations read?

3. List the things we are told to put away (v. 31).

4. On what basis are we told to forgive one another?

5. In what sense is anger involuntary?

6. In what sense do we have control over anger?

7. How are we tempted to shirk our responsibility in relation to anger?

8. How does "sin not" tell us that anger is a dangerous emotion?

9. What are the things that commonly make us angry?

10. Describe different kinds of anger and its expressions.

11. How have modern psychologists encouraged people to deal with their anger? What basis do they have for their reasoning? What is wrong with these suggestions?

12. Find as many verses as you can that encourage us to control our anger. What do you learn from these verses about anger? What is the difference between controlling anger and anger controlling us?

13. Why is anger that is carried over so dangerous?

14. What does the Bible say to do to avoid this?

15. What are some of the sins that attend bitterness?

16. What are the effects of bitterness?

17. How do people carry over their anger beyond one day?

18. What is the devil's attitude toward anger carried over? What is the attitude of the Holy Spirit toward anger?

> *Follow peace with all men, and holiness, without which no man shall see the Lord: Looking diligently lest any man fail of the grace of God; lest any root of bitterness springing up trouble you, and thereby many be defiled.* Hebrews 12:14, 15.

OBSERVATION #4: *Bitterness works under cover, like a root.*

Bitterness is not only destructive, it is deceptive as well. Most people who are bitter do not believe they are. One of the reasons is because they judge themselves emotionally. No emotion can be retained indefinitely, so once the feelings of anger leave, many people think they have right attitudes again. But if anger stayed around long enough for bitterness to set in, the emotion may have left, but the problem is just beginning.

Bitterness is essentially a pattern of blame. The pattern begins in the mind by reviewing hurtful things that have been done. The more the hurts are reviewed, the more entrenched the pattern of blame becomes. What starts as a mental pattern eventually becomes an attitude through which other actions and situations are viewed. When a person has a bitter attitude (evidenced by a tendency to blame others), not only real hurts, but imagined hurts are added to the stockpile. Some people readily talk about these things to anyone who will listen—and to some who won't. Others try to bottle them up. But the hurts are there, and the mind feeds on them regularly.

If bitterness is not dealt with, the strength of its grip increases. Eventually, a pattern of blame becomes a person's security. The bitter person develops the mind-set of a victim. To take personal responsibility, to lose the security that others are responsible for where I am and for what I am going through, is threatening. Self-pity can become so firmly rooted that the person is comfortable only when he is miserable about someone or something.

OBSERVATION #5: *Bitterness is defiling to many.*

We have looked primarily at the effects of bitterness on a person's life. But Hebrews 12 shows us that when bitterness is allowed to grow like a root, many are defiled. It spreads into many lives, creating conflict and confusion, backbiting and bickering, misunderstanding and misrepresentation. And many people get hurt.

Murmuring and strife are the overt symptoms of bitterness. But once bitterness spreads to many, there can be numerous covert symptoms as well. Depression may result—it takes a terrific amount of emotional energy to sustain resentment. Intemperance and immorality are at times symptoms of bitterness. Young people who are bitter toward their parents, for example, may gravitate toward those things that hurt their parents. And the more their parents object, the more they may indulge in them. It is common in our world for a bitter young man to meet a bitter young woman and for them to build their relationship largely on their common grievances against their parents—and move quickly into immorality together, not realizing that their craving for each other is based at least partially on their anger toward their parents.

Another way bitterness defiles is in the passing on of negative traits. When one person is bitter toward another, he often becomes like that person in the very characteristics he despises. The focus, even though negative, produces a likeness. Children who were screamed at and vow through clenched teeth never to scream at their children end up not only screaming at their children, but doing worse things. The woman who despises another woman for her unkind remarks, becomes expert at indirect negative communication herself.

What a terrible root is this bitterness! It is time we look at how to avoid it and how to root it out.

Study Questions

1. What two things are necessary in order to see the Lord?

2. From your study of anger and bitterness so far, how are peace and holiness both destroyed through anger carried over?

3. How is bitterness described in these verses? How is it like a root?

4. Why do bitter people often not realize they are bitter?

5. How is bitterness identified? Can you list examples from the Bible of people who demonstrated bitterness?

6. Trace the progression of bitterness.

7. How does blame eventually become a person's security?

8. List overt symptoms of bitterness.

9. Describe how each of the following can be a symptom of bitterness:
   a. depression   b. intemperance
   c. immorality

(Note: Beware of carrying this too far. Not all depression or all intemperance or all immorality comes from bitterness, but it *can* be a sign of bitterness.)

10. Are there other covert symptoms of bitterness that you have observed?

11. Describe how bitterness reproduces negative traits in the person who is bitter.

> *Then said he unto the disciples, It is impossible but that offences will come: but woe unto him, through whom they come! It were better for him that a millstone were hanged about his neck, and he cast into the sea, than that he should offend one of these little ones. Take heed to yourselves: If thy brother trespass against thee, rebuke him; and if he repent, forgive him. And if he trespass against thee seven times in a day, and seven times in a day turn again to thee, saying, I repent; thou shalt forgive him. And the apostles said unto the Lord, Increase our faith.* Luke 17:1-5.
>
> *Then came Peter to him, and said, Lord, how oft shall my brother sin against me, and I forgive him? till seven times? Jesus saith unto him, I say not unto thee, Until seven times: but, Until seventy times seven.* Matthew 18:21, 22.

OBSERVATION #6: *Offenses are inevitable.*

Offenses, or stumbling blocks, are not right, but we must understand that they are in the world and we will face them. We live in a world of sin. Things are not right. People get hurt. Nobody can live a pain-free life.

OBSERVATION #7: *One of the Biblical responses to being "trespassed against" is to forgive.*

We have been seeing from the Bible that anger must be controlled and that bitterness is sinful and defiling. The Bible does not provide us with a five-step plan for controlling anger, but it does give us alternate responses. The natural response when someone trespasses against us (does something wrong against us) is to become angry. If they do it again, the natural response is to become more angry. If they do it again and again, the natural response is to become bitter. Jesus gives us an alternative. Forgive! If it happens again, forgive again. If it happens again and again, forgive again and again.

What does it mean to forgive? It means to release from obligation. Forgiveness was an economic term—it was used in relation to debts. To forgive was to wipe the record clean. We see, then, that forgiveness is exactly the opposite of bitterness. Bitterness is a pattern of blame; forgiveness is a pattern of release. Instead of collaring someone (in our minds or in our speech or with our hands), we release them. They may have been wrong, but we no longer hold them to payment or obligation. In our mind and heart, where the debt is easily reviewed, we set them free, so that we no longer may dwell on their obligation to us.

OBSERVATION #8: *Forgiveness is difficult for the natural man.*

The disciples found Jesus' call to forgive seven times amazing. "Lord, increase our faith," they exclaimed. But when Jesus told Peter later, "seventy times seven," they must have felt totally flabbergasted. We can count to seven fairly easily. But who wants to keep track until 490? That is exactly Jesus' point—don't count. Just forgive.

This is beyond us. Humans find "reasonable" forgiveness hard. "I'll forgive you this time" sounds generous in our way of thinking. To forgive without counting is out of our realm. It is not only hard, it is impossible.

To forgive as Jesus taught us to forgive requires the life of Jesus Himself. Jesus was and is the great forgiver. As the soldiers were crucifying Him, He *was saying* [the Greek indicates continuous action], "Father forgive them; for they know not what they do" (Luke 23:34). We can be assured that on this day the number of trespasses exceeded 490, but Jesus wasn't counting. He was forgiving. And He calls us to do the same.

The problem is we can't on our own.

To forgive as Jesus did requires the life of Jesus in us. As the Forgiver moves into our hearts, He first forgives us, for we stand in great need of forgiveness ourselves. As we drink from the well of His forgiveness to us, we receive the strength to forgive others.

OBSERVATION #9: *Forgiveness is an act of faith.*

The disciples responded to the Lord's teaching about forgiveness with a prayer: "Lord, increase our faith." It is a fitting request, because forgiveness is a work of faith.

When someone wrongs us, our natural focus is on that person and on his wrong. Forgiveness requires that we refocus away from the offender to God. The Bible assures us repeatedly that the Lord works in behalf of those whose heart is set on Him. He is able to overrule in the affairs of men. He can work ALL things together for our eternal good (Romans 8:28). He is able to take even the unpleasant things in our lives and use them to shape us, to make us more like Jesus, and to make us more sympathetic and understanding toward others. We do not need to know how the Lord does this. We do not need to know what good He plans to accomplish out of the hardships, hurts, and troubles He is allowing in our lives. We only need to trust Him by faith.

When we look in faith to God, we are free to forgive those who trespass against us. Indeed, until we look to God in faith, forgiveness will elude us. We may try. We may say, "I forgive you." But if we are still looking at the offender, we will struggle with harboring the offense. We must look to God. The exercise of faith in a sovereign God gives us the victory over patterns of anger and blame.

Study Questions

1. What did Jesus mean by an offense? Check the original meaning of the word. Would this include hurtful things that people do to each other?

2. Do you agree that hurts are inevitable in our world? When we say that hurts are inevitable, does that mean we approve of them?

3. What group of people did Jesus especially say we should be careful not to offend?

4. How did Jesus say we should respond to a person who trespasses against us?

5. How often in one day should we forgive a penitent person? What did the disciples say in response to Jesus' teaching?

6. What did Jesus mean by His statement, "seventy times seven"?

7. What does it mean to forgive? How was the term often used other than for handling interpersonal wrongs?

8. Why do we find forgiveness hard naturally? What limitations do we tend to place on forgiveness?

9. How did Jesus leave an example of forgiveness?

10. How can we come to the place of forgiving the way Jesus taught?

11. What is our natural focus when someone wrongs us? How does this affect our ability to forgive?

12. In what way is forgiveness an exercise of faith? What Biblical truths can we believe regarding God's sovereignty over those who wrong us? Find Scriptures besides Romans 8:28 that help us with the perspective of faith.

13. In your own words, tell how the exercise of faith changes our perspective.

> *For if ye forgive men their trespasses, your heavenly Father will also forgive you: But if ye forgive not men their trespasses, neither will your Father forgive your trespasses.*
> Matthew 6:14, 15.

OBSERVATION #10: *Those who are forgiven must forgive.*

Jesus made this point very clear with a parable (Matthew 18:23-35). A man who had been forgiven a great debt was unmerciful toward a fellow servant who owed him a minor debt. Jesus' point was that we have been forgiven an unpayable debt by our heavenly Father. We were helpless under the mountain of our sins, and God forgave us on the merits of His Son's death. Not only so, but He has given us the promise of eternal life in His presence. If we, under such a deluge of mercy and grace, go out and collar someone who does something against us, we are acting like the ungrateful servant in the parable—choking a fellow servant for a few dollars after having been forgiven several million. The response of the lord is a picture of the heavenly Father—such ungratefulness will receive no mercy.

Jesus' words are clear. Those who do not forgive one another will not be forgiven by the Father. We may raise our objections. Doesn't God forget our sins? How can He bring them back against us? Exactly what the Father does with our sins is really not our business. We who are forgiven are called to forgive.

Study Questions

1. What warning did Jesus give following the Lord's Prayer (Matthew 6)?

2. In the parable of the ungrateful servant, how much did the servant owe his lord? What was his request? What was his lord's response? How much did the second servant owe his fellowservant? What was the servant's response to him? How did the other servants feel? What was the lord's response?

3. How are we like the first servant with his unpayable debt?

4. What has the heavenly Father done?

5. How are we like the first servant when we do not forgive one another?

6. What objections might we raise regarding the conclusion of this parable?

7. If a person sees himself as the unforgiving servant in this parable, what steps could he take to find forgiveness?

APPLYING THE SCRIPTURE

1. Has anger been a problem in your life? What kind of anger do you struggle with most? Flash anger? Quiet anger? Irritation? Resentment? Describe how you typically struggle?

2. Have there been situations you have found hard to accept? Describe them. What specifically have you struggled with about the situation? To what extent have you considered that God may have

purposes for you through this situation? Does that place it in a different light?

3. Are there people you have had deep resentment toward in the past? What is your present attitude toward them? If you feel you have forgiven them, on what basis do you feel that way?

4. If you have identified bitterness in your life, complete the following:

   a. Describe the situation on paper. Tell specifically how you feel you were wronged.

   b. Lay this out before the Lord in prayer, and ask Him to show you some of His possible purposes.

   c. List these purposes as specifically as you can. Don't stop until you have listed at least ten.

   d. Write out a letter to the Lord giving Him the freedom to do all these things and any others that you have not thought about.

   e. Start a Bible study, collecting verses that assure you of God's sovereignty and His goodness to His children in trial. You may also find a character in the Bible who faced similar situations. Study his life until you have learned all the Lord wants to teach you. (See Romans 15:4.)

   f. Make a list of people who have been affected by your bitterness. Use this list as a daily prayer list. Ask yourself before you pray: How would Jesus pray for these people? Approach each prayer time with that focus.

   g. If there are people on this list that you have hurt by your bitterness, purpose to clear your conscience. Confess first of all your sinful attitude. Then confess any ways you have expressed that wrong attitude. If it seems appropriate, state briefly what the Lord is teaching you. Note: Do not attempt this step until you are sure the Lord has rooted out your bitterness and you can seek to clear your conscience *without any attempt to implicate the other party in the wrong.*

5. Are there traits your parents have had that really irritated you—you determined *not* to do these things yourself? Evaluate before the Lord whether you have had a negative focus. If you have had, ask Him to show you how to refocus from *not being* like your parents to *being* like Christ. Only Christ can deliver us from subconsciously gravitating toward a negative focus.

6. If you know someone who is bitter, what is the best way to help that person? Are there times when we cannot help someone else with a problem?

7. How have you experienced or observed the passing on of anger from one generation to the next? For further study in this, see some of the events surrounding the transfer of the kingdom from Saul to David. Saul sowed seeds of bitterness that showed up years later.

PART III
UNDERSTANDING
MY RESPONSIBILITIES

Lesson 10: Developing a Servant Heart
Lesson 11: Serving the Church
Lesson 12: Reaching the Lost

"Simon, son of Jonas, lovest thou me? . . . Feed my lambs. . . . feed my sheep" (John 21:15, 16). This interchange between Jesus and Peter was charged with meaning and feeling beyond what we can easily recapture. Peter had denied Jesus. Jesus had died, had risen again, and had appeared to His disciples several times. Now, Peter had gone fishing for reasons we can only guess at, and Jesus had appeared to His night-weary, bewildered, but believing disciples with a miraculously prepared breakfast. He singles out Peter with this poignant question, thrice-repeated, "Lovest thou me?" and follows it with the commission, "Feed my sheep."

Here is Peter—so like us in weakness, in spite of having been discipled—and Jesus gives him a work to do. The disciple is called to disciple others.

This is the pattern the Master established. As we grow in our spiritual walk with Him, we are to become agents helping others. The blessings we receive are turned into responsibilities.

The three lessons that follow explore the responsibilities that come to us as we walk this road with Jesus and His people. All who sit at His feet must sooner or later learn to take the hand of others—lift the young, strengthen the weak, nurture the lambs, and feed the sheep. Every disciple of Jesus becomes a member in His great body, and as a member, he must learn to make his contribution, take his responsibility, and share of his time and energy for the good of others and for the glory of Christ.

Developing a
Servant Heart

INTRODUCTION

Self-centeredness has always stood crosswise to genuine discipleship. Since serving is a very integral part of discipleship, we may be assured that self will oppose the path of true service, sticking up its head for recognition, balking at following instructions, disdaining certain duties, complaining that others are not doing their fair share, offended at the slightest suggestion of criticism, and offended if a word of thanks is missed or goes to another person. As Christians, we would not likely have the nerve to stand and say, "Here am I, serve me," but often that is exactly what we intend when we have an opportunity to do something in the church or the community.

Disciples of Jesus are called to repent of self, whether it wears filthy clothes or beautiful religious garb; we are called to kneel before the majesty of the Lord of Hosts until we see ourselves utterly undone. When the coals from His altar have touched our self-centered lips and purged our self-centered ambitions, we are ready to say with Isaiah, humbly and genuinely,

"Here am I, send me". (See Isaiah 6:1-8.)

PERSONAL INVENTORY

1. In what specific ways are you serving God's people?

2. Are there things the church has asked you to do that you resent (or have resented)? Exactly why have you resented this? (Did you feel unqualified? Did you feel that others could do it better? Did you feel that it was a task no one else wanted? Did you want to be free from obligation?)

3. Are there people in the church whose job you wish you had?

4. Have you prayed for the Lord's direction in how to better serve in His kingdom? Have you offered yourself to Him for any service He wishes to assign to you?

5. Who in the Bible are outstanding examples of servants? What qualities do they have that you admire?

SCRIPTURAL BACKGROUND

Ye know that the princes of the Gentiles exercise dominion over them, and they that are great exercise authority upon them. But it shall not be so among you: but whosoever will be great among you, let him be your minister; and whosoever will be chief among you, let him be your servant: Even as the Son of man came not to be ministered unto, but to minister, and to give his life a ransom for many. Matthew 20:25-28.

Behold, as the eyes of servants look unto the hand of their masters, and as the eyes of a maiden unto the hand of her mistress; so our eyes wait upon the Lord our God, until that he have mercy upon us. Psalm 123:2.

And whatsoever ye do, do it heartily, as to the Lord, and not unto men; knowing that of the Lord ye shall receive the reward of the inheritance: for ye serve the Lord Christ. Colossians 3:23, 24.

I beseech you therefore, brethren, by the mercies of God, that ye present your bodies a living sacrifice, holy, acceptable unto God, which is your reasonable service. And be not conformed to this world: but be ye transformed by the renewing of your mind, that ye may prove what is that good, and acceptable, and perfect, will of God. Romans 12:1, 2.

Let this mind be in you, which was also in Christ Jesus: Who, being in the form of God, thought it not robbery to be equal with God: But made himself of no reputation, and took upon him the form of a servant, and was made in the likeness of men: And being found in fashion as a man, he humbled himself, and became obedient unto death, even the death of the cross. Philippians 2:5-8.

If I then, your Lord and Master, have washed your feet; ye also ought to wash one another's feet. For I have given you an example, that ye should do as I have done to you. John 13:14, 15.

So likewise ye, when ye shall have done all those things which are commanded you, say, We are unprofitable servants: we have done that which was our duty to do. Luke 17:10.

UNDERSTANDING THE SCRIPTURES

> *Ye know that the princes of the Gentiles exercise dominion over them, and they that are great exercise authority upon them. But it shall not be so among you: but whosoever will be great among you, let him be your minister; and whosoever will be chief among you, let him be your servant: Even as the Son of man came not to be ministered unto, but to minister, and to give his life a ransom for many.* Matthew 20:25-28.

OBSERVATION #1: A servant heart is not natural to us; our inclination is to rule.

The setting for these instructions of Jesus included an ambitious mother, two aspiring disciples, and ten indignant disciples. None of them had yet the heart of a true servant. The mother wanted her sons in high places, not lowly. Her two sons wanted the same. And the ten were upset likely because the aspirations of these two mirrored their own secret feelings. *(The audacity! To ask to sit on the right and on the left hand of the Messiah! So they want to be lords over us, too! The upstarts! They don't deserve it any more than we do.)* Whatever were the exact thoughts and mutterings of the ten, their hearts were no more inclined toward true servanthood than the hearts of the two.

Our natural inclination is to want to be first in line, to be on the top of the pile, to be looked up to by others for our position, to be able to tell others to do what pleases us, rather than them telling us what to do. We naturally disdain the low rank, look down on work that has no distinction, and avoid putting ourselves at the call of others.

To develop a servant heart means something needs to happen in us that causes us to live above our natural inclinations. That something is both negative and positive: negative, in that self must die; positive, in that a new nature must emerge out of our living union with Jesus. The old "me first" mentality must be replaced with the new "Jesus first" and "I live for the good of others" mentality.

Because something is unnatural for us does not mean it will be unenjoyable. Servanthood, in the manner of Jesus, is in fact rich with meaning, purpose, and joy.

Study Questions

1. Check the context of this incident. At what stage in Jesus' ministry did this occur?

2. With His impending crucifixion, Jesus no doubt had weighty things to think about. What does His patient response to the disciples teach us about servanthood?

3. How might the disciples have ministered to Jesus at this time?

4. Can you think of Biblical examples of the Gentile concept of servanthood?

5. How do these examples stand in contrast to the life of Jesus?

> *Behold, as the eyes of servants look unto the hand of their masters, and as the eyes of a maiden unto the hand of her mistress; so our eyes wait upon the Lord our God, until that he have mercy upon us.* Psalm 123:2.
>
> *And whatsoever ye do, do it heartily, as to the Lord, and not unto men; knowing that of the Lord ye shall receive the reward of the inheritance: for ye serve the Lord Christ.* Colossians 3:23, 24.

OBSERVATION #2: *The focus of a servant spirit is ultimately on God.*

The actual service of Jesus' followers is usually among people—taking time and doing tangible acts of kindness and love. But ultimately, we do not serve people; we serve God. People will change. People will sometimes be unattractive, undeserving, demanding, and thankless. If we serve people, we will soon be given over to confusion, compromise, frustration, and burnout.

Our eyes must be on the Master. What He says, we say. Where He sends, we go. What He commands, we do. He is the One on whom we wait. Our delight is in knowing and doing His will. Our minds and hearts are set on discerning His purposes, extending His kingdom, and accomplishing the work He entrusts to us. From Him come our orders and from Him comes our satisfaction in doing them. To Him our lives have been given and to Him goes all the glory forever. "For in him we live, and move, and have our being" (Acts 17:28).

Study Questions

1. Consider the Lord-servant relationship described in Psalm 123:2. What can the Lord expect from His servants? What can the servants expect from their Lord?

2. How does a focus on serving the Lord change the perspective for those serving earthly masters?

3. Can you give Biblical examples of a person trying to serve people instead of God?

4. What were the results?

I beseech you therefore, brethren, by the mercies of God, that ye present your bodies a living sacrifice, holy, acceptable unto God, which is your reasonable service. And be not conformed to this world: but be ye transformed by the renewing of your mind, that ye may prove what is that good, and acceptable, and perfect, will of God. Romans 12:1, 2.

OBSERVATION #3: True servanthood requires a total yielding to the will of God.

A servant heart is a yielded heart. It has gone to the altar and is wholly consecrated to the Lord. This does not mean it does what everyone demands of it. It does not mean the servant is continually under overload, trying to do more than he can and feeling guilty that there is always work to do. It does mean that he is fully and unreservedly at the call of God, that the only reasonable response to God's will is a ready, humble yes.

Servants who have been to the altar have an inner brokenness. The stubbornness, the self-will, the self-aspiring marks of the ego have passed into the fire and have gone up in smoke; and the spirit that has come through the flames is pure. There is an earnestness in the service and yet a meekness in the manner in which it is done. There is a quietness and humility in the servant and yet a strength and certainty.

Yieldedness at the altar of God is an absolute surrender. It is not the surrender of a particular item. It is not merely quitting a certain carnal activity. It is not confessing an obvious attitude of carnality. One may do any or all of these and still on the bottom line retain control. The man on God's altar yields the whole life. Every item, every activity, every attitude comes under the sway of God because the whole life is given up as a living sacrifice.

Those who try to serve the Lord and His church without the altar experience will be frustrated and they will be frustrating. They may offer themselves for ministry, and they may know the right words, but there is a giveaway in the heart. Underneath the words, behind the lip service are the marks of the unbroken self-life—an unbending spirit, a critical attitude, an indifference to spiritual growth, an independence in brotherhood, a resistance to authority, a personal agenda to pursue in the "ministry."

For those who are serious about serving God, *there is no substitute for the altar.*

Study Questions

1. What is the significance of giving ourselves as a "living sacrifice"?

2. How do other translations render "reasonable service," and what does this tell us about service?

3. How do the following expressions bear upon service?

   a. "be not conformed to this world"

   b. "be transformed by the renewing of your mind"

4. List the three things that are said about the will of God.

5. Why is it that "proving" is necessary for us to discover that the will of God is this way?

Let this mind be in you, which was also in Christ Jesus: Who, being in the form of God, thought it not robbery to be equal with God: But made himself of no reputation, and took upon him the form of a servant, and was made in the likeness of men: And being found in fashion as a man, he humbled himself, and became obedient unto death, even the death of the cross. Philippians 2:5-8.

If I then, your Lord and Master, have washed your feet; ye also ought to wash one another's feet. For I have given you an example, that ye should do as I have done to you. John 13:14, 15.

OBSERVATION #4: A true servant of God is humble.

Service may easily be used for personal advantage—to gain status, to build reputation, to influence decisions, or to control other people. The servant of the Lord serves for love and for the glory of his Master.

How easy it is to be sidetracked! When the servant has done the will of God, he is tempted to dwell on his accomplishments. When he has been humble and unassuming, he is tempted to smile with secret satisfaction on his humble manner. When he has been faithful, he is tempted to view that as giving him certain rights with God or greater clout among his fellow servants.

Nothing substitutes for a focus on the glory and worthiness of the Lord. That alone will keep a servant humble, and that is fully enough.

OBSERVATION #5: A servant is obedient.

Some service is hard. Some tasks are such that our natural inclination is to shrink from them. As Christians, we glory in the cross of Jesus, but for Jesus, it was agony. And every follower of Jesus, every servant of God, will face tests of obedience. We will struggle sometimes with accepting the will of God.

It is all right to groan in the garden, as long as we emerge willing to bear the cross. The servant may pray for the situation to change, he may legitimately ask for someone else to do the work, but only if he concludes his prayer with the words of resignation, "Nevertheless, not my will but Thine be done." The bottom line is always "Yes, Lord."

OBSERVATION #6: *Jesus is our perfect example as a servant.*

Every teaching on true servanthood is exemplified in the life of our Lord. He kept His focus on the Father. He was totally yielded to the Father's will. He was humble. He was obedient.

The night Jesus washed His disciples' feet, He gave them a tangible demonstration of servanthood. He laid aside His robe, took the towel, and washed their feet. What a parallel to His whole lifework! He laid aside the glory of deity to become a man, took up the ministry of walking up and down the roads and through the towns of humanity, and with His hands He touched the sick and sinful and brought healing.

Then He says simply but powerfully, "Do as I have done." Before that example, what robes dare we hang onto? What roads do we have reason to refuse? What people are too low, too vile, or too backward for our service?

Study Questions

1. List as many characteristics as you can of a good servant.

2. Can you find an incident in Jesus' life that matches each of your answers to the above question?

3. What attitudes in us are hindrances to a servant spirit?

4. List examples of God's servants who were obedient unto death.

5. Reviewing the list (for Question #4), what did these people have in common, and in what ways did their situations vary?

> *So likewise ye, when ye shall have done*
> *all those things which are commanded you,*
> *say, We are unprofitable servants: we have*
> *done that which was our duty to do.* Luke
> 17:10.

OBSERVATION #7: Service, no matter how noble or how much superior to that of others, does not put God in debt to us.

One of the traps of effective service is that it can make us uppity in the church. We observe that we do more than Brother Joe, and we observe furthermore that we do it better than anyone we know, and we observe in addition that we have done it longer than anyone else, and we observe beside all this that people don't appreciate what we have done.

We are ready to set a few things straight. In such huffing around, we do well to sit at the feet of Jesus again for some solid discipleship. When the disciple has done everything he possibly could for his entire lifetime in the best way possible—when he has done all that and more—he has done only his duty. His service does not make him eligible for heaven; only Jesus can do that. His service does not obligate God to do anything for him; God acts toward us out of His own mercy and upon the merits of His Son Jesus.

Does this mean our service means nothing to God? No. It is our reasonable response, and it is an important one, but our service can never obligate God. If a billionaire gave a starving bootblack five million dollars, could the bootblack earn the gift by blacking the rich man's shoes? If he polished them until they shone like chrome, he could never by his service change the reality that the gift of five million dollars was an act of mercy. So with us and God. We may shine His shoes for our entire lifetime, but in the glory of what God has done for us through His Son, we will wisely confess, "We are servants who have cost God millions more than we will ever give back by our service." Hallelujah! The glory be to Him!

Study Questions

1. What teaching was the context for Jesus' statement in Luke 17:10?

2. How is the reasoning of this parable similar to the reasoning of the parable in Matthew 18:23-35?

3. What are the consequences of developing haughty ideas about our service? How will this affect our thoughts toward God? How will it affect our thoughts and actions toward our fellowmen?

APPLYING THE SCRIPTURES

1. How do "Gentile concepts" of servanthood crop up in the church? What is the best way to go about helping "Gentile servants" become more Christlike?

2. What are Biblical motivations for service? How does motivation affect the quality of the service?

3. What are the characteristics of a person serving people instead of serving God? How should a church leader respond when he sees people servers in the congregation? How should the people in the congregation respond when they see people servers in the pulpit?

4. When we see carnal servant attitudes in ourselves, how do we go about developing a true servant spirit? In other words, how do we move from being proud to being humble, from being jealous to being generous, from being a people server to being a God server, etc.?

5. What are practical ways we can exercise humility?

6. What happens when our service is not geared toward genuine need? What is wrong when we try to serve people and they don't want our service? Is it ever right to push our service onto others?

7. What happens when service becomes an end in itself? Is it possible for people to be more devoted to their ministry than to God?

8. How much should rewards enter our minds and motivate service? Is it wrong for our hope of heaven, for example, to inspire our service? Is it wrong to be pleased when our service is appreciated? How do we graciously give and receive approval for service without fostering pride?

Lesson 11

Serving the Church

INTRODUCTION

This lesson carries the concepts in Lesson 10 forward into the church. Having a servant heart is not an end in itself. We want to understand servanthood and think servant thoughts and have a servant heart so that the church is built up, and we are bringing glory to our Lord.

Serving in the church will be meaningful to us only inasmuch as the church is meaningful. High views of the church will make service a privilege—a calling from the Lord; and high views of the church will also bring certain character qualities into focus, qualities such as love, faithfulness, and humility. Low views of the church are always accompanied by high levels of individuality and independence, and they turn service into a means to find position, a method of political maneuvering among office holders, or a means of self-expression.

PERSONAL INVENTORY

1. What is your honest view of the church? Is your attitude one of respect? Ho-hum complacency? Cynicism? Other?

2. Do you have a heartfelt love for the brothers and sisters in your local fellowship? How has that found expression in the past week? Month? Year?

3. How do you view responsibilities given to you in the church? Have you done your best?

4. If you were to meet Jesus today, would you feel comfortable with what time, energy, and resources you have put into His church?

SCRIPTURAL BACKGROUND

By love serve one another. Galatians 5:13.

Though I speak with the tongues of men and of angels, and have not charity, I am become as sounding brass, or a tinkling cymbal. And though I have the gift of prophecy, and understand all mysteries, and all knowledge; and though I have all faith, so that I could remove mountains, and have not charity, I am nothing. And though I bestow all my goods to feed the poor, and though I give my body to be burned, and have not charity, it profiteth me nothing. 1 Corinthians 13:1-3.

As every man hath received the gift, even so minister the same one to another, as good stewards of the manifold grace of God. If any man speak, let him speak as the oracles of God; if any man minister, let him do it as of the ability which God giveth: that God in all things may be glorified through Jesus Christ, to whom be praise and dominion for ever and ever. Amen. 1 Peter 4:10, 11.

Now there are diversities of gifts, but the same Spirit. . . . But the manifestation of the Spirit is given to every man to profit withal. For to one is given by the Spirit the word of wisdom; to another the word of knowledge by the same Spirit. . . . But all these worketh that one and the selfsame Spirit, dividing to every man severally as he will. But covet earnestly the best gifts. . . . 1 Corinthians 12:4-11, 31.

Even so ye, forasmuch as ye are zealous of spiritual gifts, seek that ye may excel to the edifying of the church. . . . How is it then, brethren? when ye come together, every one of you hath a psalm, hath a doctrine, hath a tongue, hath a revelation, hath an interpretation. Let all things be done unto edifying. 1 Corinthians 14:12, 26.

Wherefore, brethren, look ye out among you seven men of honest report, full of the Holy Ghost and wisdom, whom we may appoint over this business. But we will give ourselves continually to prayer, and to the ministry of the word. Acts 6:3, 4.

As they ministered to the Lord, and fasted, the Holy Ghost said, Separate me Barnabas and Saul for the work whereunto I have called them. And when they had fasted and prayed, and laid their hands on them, they sent them away. Acts 13:2, 3.

For the body is not one member, but many. If the foot shall say, Because I am not the hand, I am not of the body; is it therefore not of the body? . . . And the eye cannot say unto the hand, I have no need of thee: nor again the head to the feet, I have no need of you. . . . That there should be no schism in the body; but that the members should have the same care one for another. And whether one member suffer, all the members suffer with it; or one member be honoured, all the members rejoice with it. 1 Corinthians 12:14, 15, 21, 25, 26.

UNDERSTANDING THE SCRIPTURE

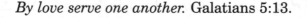

By love serve one another. Galatians 5:13.

Though I speak with the tongues of men and of angels, and have not charity, I am become as sounding brass, or a tinkling cymbal. And though I have the gift of prophecy, and understand all mysteries, and all knowledge; and though I have all faith, so that I could remove mountains, and have not charity, I am nothing. And though I bestow all my goods to feed the poor, and though I give my body to be burned, and have not charity, it profiteth me nothing. 1 Corinthians 13:1-3.

OBSERVATION #1: *Love must be the motivating force of all serving in the church.*

The Galatian churches bickered over the importance of circumcision. The church at Corinth bickered over church leaders, and they seemed bent on having spectacular gifts and using them for show in their meetings. To both of these groups Paul spoke clearly of the importance of love. Without love, doctrinal tangles will become a means of "biting and devouring" one another—even those who are doctrinally right, without love, become wrong. Without love, service becomes the means of lording. Strip love from the heart, and we strip all meaning and benefit from the service.

What is the opposite of love? Not always is it hate. The opposite of love as a motivation is self-centeredness. We had better settle it immediately and unequivocally. No matter how talented or trained or charming a person is, if he has not love, he is of no spiritual benefit in the church of Jesus Christ.

Love is a commitment to the eternal good of others. Love for our brothers and sisters is inseparably linked to a devotion to Jesus Christ. Jesus is our Lord and Saviour. We love Him because He first loved us, and because He has shed forth His love upon us, we also love all those who have likewise been redeemed by His love. He who says he loves God but has a fixation on himself instead of a love for others is a liar. He is only fooling himself. Self-centered people cannot love God, and they cannot serve effectively in the church. Their words and their talents and their deeds are spiritually empty and barren.

Study Questions

1. Look up the context of Galatians 5:13. What happens when we do not serve in love?

2. How might one follow the flesh instead of the Spirit in service? (Consider such service as a Sunday school teacher, a school board member, a song leader, a minister, or a missionary.)

3. Is it possible to exercise a spiritual gift without love, or was Paul writing hypothetically in 1 Corinthians 13?

4. What are the positive evidences of love found in 1 Corinthians 13, and what are the negative evidences (the things charity does not do)? Make two lists and try to imagine a servant in the church having one or the other. How would it affect his service?

> *As every man hath received the gift, even so minister the same one to another, as good stewards of the manifold grace of God. If any man speak, let him speak as the oracles of God; if any man minister, let him do it as of the ability which God giveth: that God in all things may be glorified through Jesus Christ, to whom be praise and dominion for ever and ever. Amen.* 1 Peter 4:10, 11.

OBSERVATION #2: Serving in the church is to be according to gifts God has given by His Spirit.

He who speaks in the church must not speak his own mind. He must speak as one whose speaking is under the control of and anointed with the unction of the Holy Spirit. He who serves in any way (whether speaking, discerning, administrating, or doing) is to be serving with eyes and ears, hands and heart tuned to the Holy Spirit. He who serves in the church by the Holy Spirit's anointing will bear the evidence of the Holy Spirit in all he does: love, joy, peace, longsuffering, gentleness, goodness, faith, meekness, and temperance.

In the New Testament, the Holy Spirit always stands opposite to the flesh. Those who serve under the anointing of the Spirit must have crucified the flesh with its affections and lusts. In the flesh we may have natural abilities—we may have eloquence, we may have a quick mind, we may have organizational ability. But if we are not graced by the gifts of the Holy Spirit, we are not equipped to serve the church. The Holy Spirit may anoint and use natural abilities, but He may also anoint and use our weaknesses.

OBSERVATION #3: Serving the church by the anointing of the Holy Spirit will bring glory to God.

The anointing of the Holy Spirit is effectual in ways beyond explanation. Gifted words, gifted minds, and gifted workings will accomplish the seeming impossible. Barriers are broken down, mountains are moved, stony hearts are softened, plans of the enemy are thwarted, and lives of people are transformed when the Holy Spirit has charge of His anointed servants. This work is for the good of God's people, but it is not for their glory. To the Father and His Son goes the glory. Spirit-anointed service will humble true servants and generate praise in their assembly.

Study Questions

1. What is the definition of a steward? Of what are we to be stewards?

2. What is the tie between the Greek word translated "grace" and the Greek word translated "gift," and what insights does this give us regarding spiritual gifts?

3. How are the gifts of the Spirit related to the fruit of the Spirit? What contradictions would result from one without the other?

4. What is the relationship between natural abilities and spiritual gifts? What dangers are there in confusing the two?

5. How might God work through one's natural weaknesses? Are there Scriptural examples of this?

> *Now there are diversities of gifts, but the same Spirit. . . . But the manifestation of the Spirit is given to every man to profit withal. For to one is given by the Spirit the word of wisdom; to another the word of knowledge by the same Spirit. . . . But all these worketh that one and the selfsame Spirit, dividing to every man severally as he will. But covet earnestly the best gifts. . . .* 1 Corinthians 12:4-11, 31.

> *Even so ye, forasmuch as ye are zealous of spiritual gifts, seek that ye may excel to the edifying of the church. . . . How is it then, brethren? when ye come together, every one of you hath a psalm, hath a doctrine, hath a tongue, hath a revelation, hath an interpretation. Let all things be done unto edifying.*
> 1 Corinthians 14:12, 26.

OBSERVATION #4: Spiritual gifts are diverse; each member has a gift, but no member has them all.

When the Holy Spirit came upon the assembled believers, He divided out the "manifold grace" or the spiritual gifts. Each member was included in this—there is no dead wood in the church. But no one member has all the gifts. Each one does his part, even as the members of our natural body. The eye sees, the ear hears, the foot walks, the hand works, the tongue speaks. Thus every member is important, but no member is all-important. Every member contributes his part, but no member does it all.

OBSERVATION #5: The effect of the gifts operating by the Spirit will be a Spirit-filled body of believers.

When the Spirit of God has His way in the church, the effect is that of a working together of the whole body. This is probably the most overlooked reality of the work of the Spirit today. Many teach the importance of being Spirit-filled. Many are interested in discerning and exercising their gifts. Many speak of what

God can do through the Spirit-filled man or woman. All of this has its place. Every member is important. But the emphasis in the New Testament is not so much on what God can do through the Spirit-filled person as it is on what He can do through the Spirit-filled assembly. The Spirit of God is given to the church to make it function effectively as the body of Christ.

Spirit-filled members, then, will have an immediate sense of humility as they see themselves as only one part of the Holy Spirit's purpose and operation. What is the eye outside of the body? Or the ear or the hand? Only in union with the body is any member significant. And only with the help of the whole body is it truly useful. Even so, members of Christ's body who are given spiritual gifts function only in cooperation with the other gifted members. Spirit-filled men and women will be humbled by their need of one another, by the blessing of being part of a much larger work to which each is able to contribute only a fraction.

By this unified working together, the glory goes clearly to the Head. The building and extending of the church is not the work of any one man or woman, but the work of the Spirit, energizing and moving in each member to do the will of Christ the Head.

OBSERVATION #6: *Spiritual gifts vary in importance; those gifts that build the church are to be esteemed.*

Spiritual gifts are given for a variety of reasons. Whatever is needed for the building of the church is available in the resources of God. Some work in the church was foundational—it was necessary at the beginning. The apostolic gifts, for example, were foundational. God gave special revelations and signs through the apostles. For years the living apostles guided the church. Much of their teaching and their revelations were recorded either by themselves or by companions close to them. We have these revelations preserved in what we know as the New Testament writings. These writings continue to be the rule of life and faith for the church. Furthermore, we view these as complete; the Gospel message was "once [for all] delivered unto the saints" (Jude 3), and to add to or take from this Gospel is heresy, attended with a curse (Galatians 1:6-9).

In writing to the Corinthians, the Apostle Paul points out that they were wrong in all seeking one gift—they seemed to want the gift of tongues above all. Paul told them the spiritual gifts that best build the church are the ones to be esteemed and sought after. But even those must be sought only in the context of fervent love for the church (Chapter 13), not for personal interests.

Study Questions

1. List Biblical purposes for spiritual gifts. Then make a list of unworthy motivations for having and exercising spiritual gifts.

2. List the spiritual gifts in 1 Corinthians 12 and tell how each has been useful in building the church.

3. How does the concept of the "body" help each member to have the right perspective of his spiritual gift? What is the importance of humility in the exercise of a spiritual gift?

4. In 1 Corinthians 14, tongues and prophecy are held in contrast. What gifts besides prophecy are especially necessary for the ongoing building of the church? What gifts besides tongues may have more limited or occasional use?

> *Wherefore, brethren, look ye out among you seven men of honest report, full of the Holy Ghost and wisdom, whom we may appoint over this business. But we will give ourselves continually to prayer, and to the ministry of the word.* Acts 6:3, 4.
>
> *As they ministered to the Lord, and fasted, the Holy Ghost said, Separate me Barnabas and Saul for the work whereunto I have called them. And when they had fasted and prayed, and laid their hands on them, they sent them away.* Acts 13:2, 3.

OBSERVATION #7: *Some members in the church are set apart for special tasks and responsibilities.*

The apostles, we have noted, had a foundational work to do in the church. To that work, they gave themselves wholeheartedly and sacrificially. From that work, they would not be deterred. When need arose for giving oversight to the distribution of material things, the apostles saw that this was work for someone else. They appointed seven men. Notice that although the work of these men was the management of material things, the qualifications say nothing about things material. The men were to have an honorable reputation (literal meaning of "honest report"). They were to be filled with the Holy Spirit. And they were to be men of wisdom.

When there was a specific responsibility given to members—especially an ongoing responsibility in the brotherhood—the church leaders gave a special charge to these members. Thus, deacons, elders, and evangelists were appointed (by what methods we are not always told). The hands of church leaders were laid on them, apparently calling for spiritual gifts to enable the one(s) chosen. (See 1 Timothy 4:14.) These chosen ones then were charged to be faithful in the work appointed to them.

OBSERVATION #8: Although no prescribed methods are given for appointing members to offices, the methods employed in the early church honored enduring principles.

First, those selected needed to meet godly criteria. They were not selected at random. The qualities mentioned emphasize spiritual maturity, and to require these qualities in candidates calls for sound judgment and solid leadership in the appointing process.

Second, the selection process seems to have included the church body. The apostles did not hand pick the seven men who "served tables." They involved the church in the selection, and the men came from the assembled believers whom the apostles had been discipling for an extended time.

Third, the work of selecting members for particular responsibilities was accompanied with prayer and fasting, a calling on the Lord for direction. Through fasting and prayer, the leaders at Antioch discerned that the Lord wanted Paul and Barnabas to set forth in evangelism. Through fasting and prayer, Paul and Barnabas later ordained elders in the congregations they had newly established. (See Acts 14:23.) This is clearly not to be a bid for position by candidates. Ordination to minister in the church must never descend to a political maneuvering between rival parties, prominent families, or aspiring, outspoken members. Ministry in the church is a calling of God, and it is to be taken up with humility, love for the church, and reverence toward God.

OBSERVATION #9: *A special call to ministry is confirmed through the church.*

Paul had been called as an apostle to the Gentiles the day he met the Lord on the road to Damascus. He began to testify of the Lord's grace immediately after his baptism, and he spoke readily to believers and unbelievers. His ordination to go as an evangelist, however, came years later (at least ten years later, perhaps as many as fourteen). Thus, while his call came to him personally from the Lord, his commission came through the church.

Those today who sense a call from the Lord of the church must trust the Lord to reveal to the church the timing. Various men in the Scriptures reflect the problems that result from running ahead of God, and others the wisdom of waiting on the Lord through years of preparation after receiving a call (consider Moses and David, for example). Paul spent two years in the desert, and then more years in Tarsus. By waiting on the Lord and honoring the direction of the church, Paul became an effective servant.

Study Questions

1. List the qualifications for the men chosen in Acts 6, and tell how each qualification was necessary for the work assigned to the men.

2. Describe the function of these men as accurately as you can from the text. Is there need for such men today in the church?

3. From what work did the apostles not want to be distracted? What might have been the effects of the apostles neglecting their work?

4. What is the meaning of the phrase "ministered to the Lord" (Acts 13:2)?

5. Find the occasions in the Book of Acts where ordinations took place. (See Chapters 1, 6, and 13.) What methods were used? What principles were honored? What different offices were in view?

> *For the body is not one member, but many. If the foot shall say, Because I am not the hand, I am not of the body; is it therefore not of the body? . . . And the eye cannot say unto the hand, I have no need of thee: nor again the head to the feet, I have no need of you. . . . That there should be no schism in the body; but that the members should have the same care one for another. And whether one member suffer, all the members suffer with it; or one member be honoured, all the members rejoice with it.* 1 Corinthians 12:14, 15, 21, 25, 26.

OBSERVATION #10: We do not follow Jesus alone; every member needs the church for strength, wisdom, and spiritual nurture.

The other side of serving in the church is that every member needs the service of the other members. Even as the hand and the foot or any other member of our natural body could not function apart from the body, so Christians are never intended to live their lives independent of the brotherhood. Sometimes Christians develop ideas or plans that fit only themselves, ideas that set them apart and make them unwilling to be involved in the brotherhood. Independent actions and aloof attitudes sometimes may rise from unfortunate experiences—people sometimes get hurt or offended in the church. Or they may observe inconsistencies in other members or in the group as a whole.

The truth is, however, that God never intended any one member to be the church in himself (the church is an assembly, not the private enterprise of an individual). When a member has concerns for another member or for the group as a whole, he must keep in mind his limited insight as one member alone—he needs his brothers and sisters to see the issue properly, he needs the strength that comes from unity with them to stand against Satan and the world, and he needs their nurturing to grow properly. Much of the shaping and spiritual development of members comes in the interaction with brothers and sisters in the body of Christ. This interaction will include encouragement, working together, submitting one to another, and helping one another. Without this, no member can survive spiritually.

Anytime a member has ideas or plans that set him in opposition to the church, causing him to be critical of the church and to act independently, that member has lost his sense of needing the body. Furthermore, if he does not submit to his need of his brothers and sisters, he cannot be a true servant.

Study Questions

1. Look at the questions asked in 1 Corinthians 12:15-20. These are rhetorical questions, but what answer would you give to each one?

2. What would be the effect of a body member trying to act independently? By analogy, what is the effect of a church member acting independently?

3. How does the "body" concept of the church help us to understand the nurture of each member? the strength of each member?

4. How does the overall working together of a group affect each individual member? And how does the lack of cooperation of one member affect the group?

5. What were some of the schisms (factions) in the church at Corinth? How does the teaching in 1 Corinthians 12 address underlying problems that lead to splits?

APPLYING THE SCRIPTURES

1. What attitudes are important for serving others? How can we develop those attitudes? What should we do when we observe wrong attitudes in others in the church?

2. What are the distinctive earmarks of serving in the strength of the flesh instead of serving in the power of the Spirit? What should a minister do when he observes a member trying to serve in the strength of the flesh? What should a member do when he observes a minister trying to serve in the strength of the flesh?

3. What are some misconceptions about spiritual gifts? How do we give ourselves freely to the Holy Spirit, even to the point of Him doing among us the unexpected, and avoid the snares of sensationalism and emotionalism?

4. What is the difference between ordaining and commissioning? What might be the benefit of the church commissioning a member for a specific service?

5. How can the church be more effective in including each member in the work of the church? Are there areas of service we ought to explore more? What are the effects of having members who have no specific task to do? In what ways can members take the initiative to serve their brothers and sisters without being assigned to specific tasks?

6. What are common needs in congregations today? How can members be meeting those needs? How do well-meaning people try to serve others sometimes when their service is not needed? Can you help someone who doesn't want help? Can you help someone without that person realizing it?

7. Does everyone have a spiritual gift? If so, is this a lifelong gift, and will this be the way the person serves the church no matter where he is? Or does the Spirit give gifts according to the needs in a given time and place? Is it necessary to know exactly what spiritual gift each one has? What dangers are there in focusing on one's gift instead of focusing on the needs at hand in the church? What dangers are there in focusing on the needs at hand and ignoring whether one has the gift for meeting that need?

8. What evidences are there of independence in church members today? What happens when a member decides he doesn't need the input of the church, or when he becomes generally critical of the church? What qualities are necessary in a member when he needs to express concerns about the church? Is it possible to emphasize the body concept of the church so much that individual members suffer? What are the effects of overemphasis on group needs and group decisions?

Reaching the Lost

INTRODUCTION

We live in a sinful world. The judgment of God is already passed on this world, and the judgment is unequivocal: this world will pass away and all sinners will be cast with Satan and his hosts into eternal perdition. God has provided a way of escape through the death and resurrection of His Son, Jesus Christ. And He has commissioned all disciples of Jesus to spread the word of redemption to those who do not know. This is the Gospel—the good news of salvation through Jesus.

It is impossible to be a follower of Jesus without hearing His call to become involved in reaching the lost. Disciples will be involved in different ways. Some will be called to focus their lifework on evangelism. Some will be organizers of the work. Some will give resources to help support the work. All can share their personal testimony with those around them in one-on-one encounters. And yet, while each individual may have his part, it takes the church—the living body—to reach the lost effectively. A sinner can see Jesus in a

Christian, but the fullness of Jesus is revealed through His body.

Evangelism is more than leading people to receive Jesus; it includes "teaching them [literally, "discipling them"] to observe all things" that Jesus taught (Matthew 28:20). Reaching the lost, then, is more than getting people to confess their sinfulness; it is discipling them out of sinful practices and into the ways of God. It begins with reaching the sinner, and it continues with teaching and training him as a child of God and as a member of God's family. Jesus came "to seek and to save that which was lost" (Luke 19:10), and His church is commissioned to carry on the work in His name and by the power of His Holy Spirit.

PERSONAL INVENTORY

1. In what specific ways have you been involved in reaching the lost?

2. In what areas of evangelism do you feel a personal need? (Vision? Understanding? Methods? Opportunities? etc.)

3. When was the last time you shared your faith with an unbeliever, and how did it go?

4. What specific plans does your congregation have for reaching out with the Gospel, and what has been your involvement?

SCRIPTURAL BACKGROUND

All power is given unto me in heaven and in earth. Go ye therefore, and teach all nations, baptizing them in the name of the Father, and of the Son, and of the Holy Ghost: Teaching them to observe all things whatsoever I have commanded you: and, lo, I am with you alway, even unto the end of the world. Amen. Matthew 28:18-20.

But ye shall receive power, after that the Holy Ghost is come upon you: and ye shall be witnesses unto me both in Jerusalem, and in all Judaea, and in Samaria, and unto the uttermost part of the earth. Acts 1:8.

Now when they had gone throughout Phrygia and the region of Galatia, and were forbidden of the Holy Ghost to preach the word in Asia, After they were come to Mysia, they assayed to go into Bithynia: but the Spirit suffered them not. . . . And a vision appeared to Paul in the night; There stood a man of Macedonia, and prayed him, saying, Come over into Macedonia, and help us. And after he had seen the vision, immediately we endeavoured to go into Macedonia, assuredly gathering that the Lord had called us for to preach the gospel unto them. Acts 16:6-10.

And he gave some, apostles; and some, prophets; and some, evangelists; and some, pastors and teachers; for the perfecting of the saints, for the work of the ministry, for the edifying of the body of Christ: Till we all come in the unity of the faith, and of the knowledge of the Son of God, unto a perfect man, unto the measure of the stature of the fulness of Christ. Ephesians 4:11-13.

UNDERSTANDING THE SCRIPTURES

> *All power is given unto me in heaven and in earth. Go ye therefore, and teach all nations, baptizing them in the name of the Father, and of the Son, and of the Holy Ghost: Teaching them to observe all things whatsoever I have commanded you: and, lo, I am with you alway, even unto the end of the world. Amen.* Matthew 28:18-20.

OBSERVATION #1: Evangelism has been authorized by the risen Son of God, and it has His unwavering support.

When the Lord commissioned His disciples to go make other disciples, He did so after His earthly work of redemption had been completed. He had died and He had risen from the dead. He had conquered death and broken the power of sin and Satan. On the merits of His death and resurrection, He had received from the Father the "power"—the authority, the full rights—to be Lord of heaven and earth. By this authority, He commissioned His disciples to disciple. All the authorities in heaven must bow to this risen Son of God; all authorities on earth must bow to Him. Jesus has been given all power, and those who go forth go in His worthy name.

Those who go forth to evangelize in Jesus' name have His unwavering support. "I am with you always," the Lord says. The magnitude of that support is appreciated only when we lift our eyes to the heights to which Jesus ascended. He is Lord of all. He can command angels to attend His sent ones; He can command the hills to bring forth for their needs; He can command mountains to make a way for His disciples; He can still the storm, multiply the loaves, bless the children, curse the unproductive trees, and cleanse the corrupted temples. Thus, He did not leave us alone when He went to heaven. He is Lord of all, and by His Holy Spirit, He is with us always.

OBSERVATION #2: *Evangelism rests entirely on the redemptive work of Jesus.*

Those who evangelize have one foundation on which to build. They do not build on their credentials, they do not build on their denomination, they do not build on their heritage. They build on the redemptive work of Jesus. Jesus died and rose from the dead. The evangelist is spreading this truth, showing men and women that this work of Jesus on their behalf is fully sufficient to change their eternal destiny.

It is important to note here that the redemptive work of Jesus includes both His death and resurrection. By His death, Jesus effectively made the sacrifice so that sins can be forgiven. By His resurrection from the dead, Jesus entered into the work of living "to make intercession for us." He can save from sins past, and He can save "to the uttermost" (Hebrews 7:25). We need the Saviour's death on the cross to deliver us from the guilt of sin, and we need the Saviour's life in heaven to deliver us from the power of sin.

OBSERVATION #3: *The essential call of evangelism is to make people disciples of Jesus.*

The translation loses some of the force in the original language. The emphasis of the commission in the

English is on the first word, "Go." The Greek conveys more the idea of "going," so that the emphasis actually falls on the next imperative, "Teach!" In other words, "In your going, teach." The word translated "teach" is translated elsewhere as "disciple." In our going, we are to disciple others; that is, we are to cause them to be disciples of Jesus.

Evangelism is not something done primarily in remote areas, but rather, it is something done in the normal round of going. Wherever we go, we are under commission to make disciples. This will certainly take some to areas far away, but it will happen wherever God's children are. Every Christian is going, and every Christian is an evangelist. Every church is a mission church. As congregations grow, it is right that they reach out to other areas by sending missionaries. The mother church, however, is no less a mission church— she must continue the work of discipling people for Jesus.

OBSERVATION #4: *To disciple people means to cause them to walk according to the teachings of Jesus.*

Jesus came as a revelation of the Father. The Law revealed God in word; Jesus revealed God in life. Jesus did not destroy the Law, but rather, He showed us the full intent and purpose of God's Law. Thus, Jesus' teachings and His example become for us the expression of the Father's will for our lives. Disciples of Jesus will want to know what He said. They will study His teachings. They will view Jesus as their model for living.

Following Jesus is not merely academic, however. It is not textbook learning only. The disciple of Jesus learns to walk according to Jesus' teachings, yes; but in spirit, he learns to walk with Jesus Himself.

In discipleship, zealous people can fall into a trap on two sides by emphasizing one truth against another. Some will emphasize the teachings of Jesus as a catechism to the neglect of the living relationship with Jesus in the heart. They know the doctrine. They teach the doctrine. Outwardly they follow the doctrine. But their hearts are sterile of true life. Others (often in reaction to doctrine without life) will emphasize the inner relationship to the neglect of sound doctrine. They scoff at doctrine. They equate structured teaching, careful interpretation, and godly application with legalism. To them it matters not so much that Christians believe the same thing, but only that Christians can testify of inner life. The Christian life is left to the interpretation of every man according to his personal experience. The unfortunate result of both errors is drift from true discipleship.

The truth is that we need to know and study and live by the teachings of Jesus even while we live in spiritual union with Him. It is in living relationship with Jesus that the beauty and rightness of His teachings are made known. And it is in living by His teachings that we come to know Him better and love Him more dearly.

Study Questions

1. What is the meaning of the Greek word translated "power" in Matthew 28:18? How does it compare with the Greek word translated "power" in Acts 1:8?

2. What does "all authority" mean in relation to Jesus? How do the following passages further

help us to understand the authority that has been given to Jesus?

a. Ephesians 1:19-20   b. Philippians 2:9-11
c. Colossians 2:15

3. Read the Great Commission in several other translations. What additional insights do you receive?

4. What is the purpose of baptism in making disciples?

5. What teachings of Jesus are commonly neglected in discipleship today?

6. List examples from the New Testament that show that Jesus was "with" those who did as He instructed. What examples do you find of His authority?

> *But ye shall receive power, after that the Holy Ghost is come upon you: and ye shall be witnesses unto me both in Jerusalem, and in all Judaea, and in Samaria, and unto the uttermost part of the earth.* Acts 1:8.

OBSERVATION #5: The work of evangelism calls for the indwelling power of the Holy Spirit.

To disciple people for Jesus means they must be made alive spiritually. It also means they need spiritual growth—an ongoing inner spiritual work of sanctifying the heart and shaping the character.

Accomplishing these things involves disciplers, but the actual work is a work of God. The Apostle Paul expressed it thus, "I have planted, Apollos watered; but God gave the increase" (1 Corinthians 3:6). Every part of the work, therefore, must have the anointing and direction of the Holy Spirit. Every discipler must be filled with and empowered by the Holy Spirit.

The first disciples were told to wait in Jerusalem for the anointing. The need was all around them. The need was all the time. But the first lesson in evangelism is that it is God's work. It takes God's power. No one can bring others to Jesus apart from the power of God. No one can testify effectively without that power. No one can lead them onward in spiritual progress except God is working and moving by His power.

This is humbling. We are not sufficient for the work of evangelism. We must have God.

OBSERVATION #6: *When evangelism is empowered by the Holy Spirit, it spreads.*

Notice outward movement of Acts 1:8—Jerusalem (the birthplace of the church), Judea (the immediate surrounding area), Samaria (next-door territory, both in location and in culture), and then, out to all the world. What Jesus described here is verified in the Book of Acts. The Holy Spirit came upon the believers at Pentecost in that upper room in Jerusalem. Daily, for some time, the assembly was limited to Jerusalem—in the temple, in homes, but always under the powerful, Spirit-filled teaching of the apostles. More came to the Lord and were added to the church. As the group grew, so grew the opposition. Finally, it broke out in the stoning of Stephen and in Saul's hate-filled campaign against all followers of Jesus. The believers were scattered, and like flaming fragments of a growing fire, wherever the believers went out, they spread the Gospel. Instead of putting out the fire, the scattering only increased it. Into Judea it went, into Samaria, and then, under the direction of the Holy Spirit, it broke out into the Gentile community at Antioch, and from there Saul, converted from church hating, was sent out to evangelize in new communities. The fire spread all over Rome.

Such is the effect of the Gospel under the direction of the Spirit. It grows. It spreads. It cannot be contained under a basket, confined to one person, one family, one community, one race, or one culture. It breaks through man-made limitations and surprises our expectations. It is indeed a work of God.

OBSERVATION #7: *The Holy Spirit causes people to testify of Jesus.*

While this may seem like an obvious point by this time in our study, we pause to note this because sometimes when the Spirit is working, people get sidetracked.

"Ye shall receive power" rings pleasantly in our ears. We are drawn to power. Our eyes open when we see miracle-working demonstrations of God. Unfortunately, even very carnal people can get excited about the power described in Acts 1:8. We would like to run around doing great things and telling exciting stories.

The Holy Spirit is not impressed with the ambitions of the natural man. His work is to lift up Jesus. His empowering is for those who have renounced self and are wholly taken up with Jesus. When our desire is only to exalt Jesus, when our burden is to testify to those who have not heard, when our yearning personally is to know Him better each day, the Holy Spirit is willing to come upon us, move within us, and speak through us. He will take our words and make them trumpet blasts of the Gospel. He will take our weaknesses and turn them into powerful messages of Christ's grace. He will energize and fill and accomplish beyond our awareness, until the only reasonable response from us is "not I, but Christ."

Study Questions

1. What kind of power was promised here? How is it essential to the task of witnessing?

2. What examples can you give of people wanting power, even spiritual power, for wrong motivations? How does Acts 8:19 show this danger?

3. What does it mean to be a witness of Jesus?

4. The Greek word translated "witness" is also translated "martyr" at times. What does this add to your understanding of this promise?

5. What is your Jerusalem? Judea? Samaria?

6. Are there areas in the "uttermost part of the earth" that still need the Gospel?

7. Try to determine as clearly as you can how long the work of witnessing was largely in Jerusalem. How many years was it until the Gospel was preached in Samaria? How long was it until there was an organized effort to carry the Gospel to the Gentiles? How does the passage of years and the activity of the apostles during those years help us to understand effective evangelism today?

> *Now when they had gone throughout Phrygia and the region of Galatia, and were forbidden of the Holy Ghost to preach the word in Asia, After they were come to Mysia, they assayed to go into Bithynia: but the Spirit suffered them not. . . . And a vision appeared to Paul in the night; There stood a man of Macedonia, and prayed him, saying, Come over into Macedonia, and help us. And after he had seen the vision, immediately we endeavoured to go into Macedonia, assuredly gathering that the Lord had called us for to preach the gospel unto them.*
> Acts 16:6-10.

OBSERVATION #8: Evangelism calls for sensitivity to the Holy Spirit's direction.

We are limited in our vision. We don't know the future. We don't even know many things about the present. If we were on our own, the work of saying the right things at the right time to the right people would be largely guesswork. The Holy Spirit doesn't operate by guesswork. He knows the heart. He knows the time. He knows the words that will be effective. Those who would do the work of the Lord must have hearts and ears that are tuned to the voice of the Holy Spirit.

The Spirit's direction may sometimes go against our ideas. It sounds strange indeed to read that Paul and his companions were "forbidden of the Holy Ghost to preach the word in Asia." But God knows all things. He is always right. A woman named Lydia needed Paul a certain day by a certain river in Macedonia. An exploited slave girl needed him another day on a certain street. And a jail keeper needed to hear the Gospel at a certain time of the night. The Lord directed Paul to these people through various means, but through it all Paul could not glory in his insight—he went by the Lord's direction.

Learning to hear the inner voice of the Spirit is important for every believer. Those who are carnal are easily misled (recall Lesson 8, the section on impressions). As we walk in step with Jesus, we can trust Him to guide us.

OBSERVATION #9: Evangelism carried out under the direction of the Holy Spirit is effective.

When we are faithful in obeying the voice of the Spirit, He is faithful in doing His part. Lydia was saved, the slave girl was delivered, the jailer and his household were baptized, and a church was established at Philippi.

These results are not a tribute to Paul but to the Lord. He gives the increase.

Study Questions

1. On a map, trace out the regions of Paul's preaching activity in Acts 16:6-10. How does this area compare to his work in his first missionary journey?

2. When in Paul's ministry did he go to those regions in Asia that he was here told not to go into?

3. What new territory was opened up by the call from Macedonia?

4. List specifically the people who were brought to the Lord after Paul went into Europe. List also the places where churches were established. What do these responses tell about the wisdom of the Spirit's leading?

> *And he gave some, apostles; and some, prophets; and some, evangelists; and some, pastors and teachers; for the perfecting of the saints, for the work of the ministry, for the edifying of the body of Christ: Till we all come in the unity of the faith, and of the knowledge of the Son of God, unto a perfect man, unto the measure of the stature of the fulness of Christ.* Ephesians 4:11-13.

OBSERVATION #10: Evangelism is a function within the church that calls for the contribution of each member and cooperation of the whole body.

The work of making people disciples of Jesus is a church work. Many members have a part in the salvation and spiritual growth of any one believer. For example, a man may look back on all of the following: someone's personal testimony first brought him under conviction, another's life verified the truth of the Gospel, someone else may have given him a Gospel tract, still another person actually led him to repentance and faith in Christ, church leaders instructed him, and numerous others prayed with him, held Bible studies, gave encouragement, worked alongside of him in worship and service opportunities, and as he grew, the church assigned him spiritual responsibilities that stimulated growth. Who discipled this Christian? The answer is that the church did.

When we come to faith in Christ, we come into the assembly of believers, and every member becomes the means of nurturing, shaping, and bringing us to maturity in Christ.

May God give us not only Spirit-filled evangelists, but Spirit-filled assemblies to disciple people for Jesus till He comes.

Study Questions

1. Look at the different gifts named in Ephesians 4:11. By studying the words, write a definition for each gift and tell how that gift is necessary in the work of discipling people for Jesus.

2. From the New Testament, give several examples of each gift mentioned in Ephesians 4:11. What were the specific results of their discipling others?

3. List the goals of exercising these gifts, as described in Ephesians 4:12, 13.

4. What different words are used in this passage to describe spiritual progress? Check the meaning of these words in the original language, or read the passage in several other translations. What do you learn?

5. This passage is actually describing the maturing process of the church, not an individual Christian. How does this concept add to your understanding of the passage? In what way does a group mature spiritually? What are the results if a group stays spiritually immature?

6. Think of the church as a body. How does it take the whole church (not just an individual) to do the will of Jesus? How does it take the whole church (not just an individual) to show Jesus to the world? (See John 17:23.)

APPLYING THE SCRIPTURE

1. How can Christians sometimes lose sight of the authority of Jesus, and how does this affect the work of discipling people for Jesus? What are some ways this can be regained?

2. Paul said he became all things to all men to win them to Christ. How does this principle apply to evangelism today in America? How does it apply to Americans going to Guatemala or Haiti or Africa?

3. What methods are most effective in reaching American unbelievers? What methods are not as effective here (which may be effective in other settings)?

4. How can believers work together in evangelism and discipleship? What are ways we can sharpen vision, encourage participation, and develop skill in reaching the lost?

5. What are some essentials for the church to be effective in evangelism and discipleship? What attitudes in the church are especially harmful to the work of evangelism? Is it possible to develop a "closed-circle" mentality in a congregation in such a way that people who are seeking spiritual fellowship do not feel welcome? How does such a problem develop, and what can be done to help it?

6. How should we feel about unreached areas in our world today? What might we be doing more effectively? How might we go about making plans to reach these areas? To what extent should we join with other groups who are targeting unreached areas?

7. How can we encourage and support workers in other places? What can we do for missionaries in Central America, for example? Would there be ways to support them more effectively?

Books by John Coblentz

Christian Family Living Series

Christian Family Living
Practical, Step-by-Step Instructions From Training Toddlers to Caring for Aging Parents

God's Will for My Body—Guidance for Adolescents

Looking at Myself Before Loving Someone Else

Courtship That Glorifies God—A Biblical Approach to Dating and Engagement

Singlehood That Glorifies God—Living With Eternal Purpose

Before You Say Your Vows—Premarital Counseling— A Guide for Couples and Counselors

God's Will for Love in Marriage—Cultivating Marital Intimacy

What the Bible Says About Marriage, Divorce, and Remarriage

Victorious Living

The Upward Call—Studies in Christian Discipleship

The Victorious Life

Putting Off Anger—A Biblical Study of What Anger Is and What to Do About It

Beauty for Ashes—Biblical Help for the Sexually Abused

Music in Biblical Perspective

Are Written Standards for the Church?

Christian Light Publications, Inc., is a nonprofit, conservative Mennonite publishing company providing Christ-centered, Biblical literature including books, Gospel tracts, Sunday school materials, summer Bible school materials, and a full curriculum for Christian day schools and homeschools. Though primarily produced in English, some books, tracts, and school materials are also available in Spanish.

For more information about the ministry of CLP or its publications, or for spiritual help, please contact us at:

Christian Light Publications, Inc.
P. O. Box 1212
Harrisonburg, VA 22803-1212

Telephone—540-434-0768
Fax—540-433-8896
E-mail—info@clp.org